THE ELUSIVE FULL
RIDE SCHOLARSHIP
An Insider's Guide

MIA WENJEN AND ALISON FOLEY

THE ELUSIVE FULL RIDE SCHOLARSHIP
An Insider's Guide

MIA WENJEN AND ALISON FOLEY

The Elusive Full Ride Scholarship: An Insider's Guide

Text Copyright 2020

Text design: meadencreative.com

Cover design: meadencreative.com

First Edition: 2020

Library of Congress Control Number on File

P-ISBN: 978-1-936426-28-7

E-ISBN: 978-1-936426-29-4

Audrey Press
P.O. Box 6113
Maryville, TN 37802

Visit us at **www.audreypress.com**

Printed in the USA

DEDICATION

This book was created with the insights of parents, coaches, college athletes and college athletes-to-be with the one common goal of assisting families in the recruiting process. I want to thank you all for making this process a smoother one for so many families who will read this book. AF

To my mother, Rose Wenjen, who in her 95 years here on earth, always supported the dreams and aspirations of everyone in her life. MW

CONTENTS

INTRODUCTION

If you are a parent or a high school student reading this book, congratulations! You (or your child) are part of an elite group of athletes who play sports in high school and want to play in college. And that's amazing because the odds of playing high level sports in college are daunting. Did you know that 70% of all kids quit organized sports by age 13[1] and only 7% of high school athletes move on to college sports?[2]

According to the NCAA, "Nearly eight million students currently compete in high school athletics in the United States … with more than 480,000 [competing] as NCAA athletes… and just a select few within each sport move on to compete at the professional or Olympic level."[3]

To achieve this goal of playing sports in college, you are taking the first step in learning how the college sports recruiting process works.

You might have questions about this: am I good enough to

play for Division I, II or III colleges? When do I contact a college coach? What do I say to a college coach to express interest? How important are grades and test scores? What if college coaches don't contact me or respond to my emails? How do I present myself to college coaches in order to be recruited? When do I apply to college if I am being recruited?

It is important to know that no one path is correct for everyone. Each school and coach may handle the process differently for their prospective student-athletes (PSA).

It helps to understand the landscape of college athletic recruiting before you begin your journey. We will point you to the right sources for additional information as you prepare for this exciting, and sometimes intimidating process because being proactive can greatly increase your chance of success.

....

[1] Poll from National Alliance for Sports. Miner, Juliana M. "Why 70% of kids quit sports by age 13?" WashingtonPost.com website. 1 June 2016. Web. The Washington Post. 11 July 2019.

[2] Amanda J. Visek, Sara M. Achrati, Heater Manning, Karen McDonnell, Brandonn S. Harris, and Loretta DiPietro. The Fun Integration Theory: Towards Sustaining Children and Adolescents Sports Participation. Journal of Physical Activity and Health. 2015 March; 12(3): 424.433.

[3] "Estimated probability of competing in college athletics." NCAA.com website. Retrieved 11 July 2019 from http://www.ncaa.org/about/resources/research/estimated-probability-competing-college-athletics

Peter Kim
Head Coach Women's Soccer
Assistant Coach Men's and Women's Track and Field
Middlebury College

Focus on the real goal. The ultimate goal of the college search process is to find a place where you will be happy. It's easy to fall into the trap of choosing your school for one of many wrong reasons – division, coaches' attention/promises, etc. This may mean getting to know yourself better so that you understand what you will need to make college a fulfilling experience. It also means taking a close look at the entire campus community, not just the athletic program.

THE COLLEGE ATHLETIC RECRUITMENT PROCESS

Did you know that there are many different levels and ways to play sports in college from varsity, junior varsity, club, and intramurals? While NCAA Divisions I and II colleges as well as NAIA colleges and some junior colleges offer athletic scholarships, there are numerous ways to play sports in college and different options to fund college. Being a strong student will increase your options.

Academics First. Sports Second.

Colleges and coaches look for good students. One of the most important things to remember is to work hard and keep your grades up over the course of high school. Choosing a rigorous course load will also matter to colleges with strong academics. This demonstrates how you perform in the classroom and what type of student you are in the eyes of the Admissions counselors and directors when they review your transcript. You have to be a student first and an athlete second.

The intercollegiate athletic recruitment process is complex. The rules are different depending on the type of college and the particular sport. To make it even more complicated, the rules are continually changing.

You might have seen terms like: "I'm getting recruited by…," "she/he committed to …," "preferred walk-on," "visited," and "roster spots versus scholarship spots." These terms will all be clarified as you read through this book.

As you begin the process of selecting colleges, know that coaches are looking at you as a whole person, not solely on your athletic ability. Being a strong and well-rounded student will increase the number of schools for you to consider.

You got this! You've worked hard to achieve your best. Now is the time to showcase who you are.

John Kennaday
Head Coach Men's Varsity Golf
San Jose State

Work your network. The world is so small now that you probably have an endorsement that you may or may not know about to actually get the coach's ear. Coaches are inundated with emails about prospects not only from the prospects themselves but from recruiting services. Odds are that I'm going to get twenty emails today. And twenty tomorrow. And I will receive twenty after that. You start to turn a blind eye to that as a coach and you wait for a personal testimonial … a phone call, a connection from someone you know about the kid.

In my sport, the coach is going to be able to tell if you can play or not by the statistics and rankings.

THE FULL RIDE ATHLETIC SCHOLARSHIP

NCAA Division I and II schools provide more than $2.9 billion in athletic scholarships annually to more than 150,000 student-athletes.[4] Division III schools do not offer athletic scholarships but can offer financial aid to athletes—with the same criteria that they use for non-athletes.

Despite the $2.9 billion awarded every year, only 2% of high school students receive athletic scholarships[5], out of all NCAA Division I and II schools—including all men's and women's sports. Not all of these scholarships are full-rides either. In fact, the average scholarship is less than $11,000.[6]

For example, more than 600,000 girls competed in track and field in high school for 4,506 scholarships. These scholarships were split among 9,888 athletes and the average award was $8,105.

The numbers are similar in soccer. More than 330,000 boys played soccer in high school where there were 2,357 soccer scholarships available. These soccer scholarships were split among 6,047 students and the average award was $8,533.[7]

Basketball is another example. Just 3.3% of high school seniors playing boy's basketball will have roster positions on NCAA teams as freshmen—with or without scholarships, according to NCAA data. For girls, the figure is 3.7%. Put another way, the odds of landing a college scholarship in many major sports are lower than the chances of being admitted to Harvard, Yale, Princeton or Stanford.[8]

....

[4] "Scholarship." NCAA.com website. Retrieved 11 July 2019 from http://www.ncaa.org/student-athletes/future/scholarships

[5] "Scholarship." NCAA.com website. Retrieved 11 July 2019 from http://www.ncaa.org/student-athletes/future/scholarships

[6] Lynn O'Shaughnessy. "8 Things You Should Know About Sports Scholarships." CBSNews.com website. 20 September 2012. Retrieved 11 July 2019 from https://www.cbsnews.com/news/8-things-you-should-know-about-sports-scholarships/

[7] Lynn O'Shaughnessy. "The Odds of Getting a Sports Scholarship: Part II." TheCollegeSolution.com website. Retrieved 16 July 2019 from http://www.thecollegesolution.com/the-odds-of-getting-an-athletic-scholarship-part-ii

[8] Kelley Holland and John W. Schoen. "Think athletic scholarship are a holy grail? Think again." CNBC.com Website. 13 October 2013. Retrieved 16 July 2019 from https://www.cnbc.com/2014/10/13/think-athletic-scholarships-are-a-holy-grail-think-again.html

Sarah Dacey
Head Coach Women's Soccer
Barry University

Don't assume you will get a full scholarship!
There is a limited amount of scholarships per program and money is usually allotted in many different ways among multiple athletes. Understand that each year, the number of athletes who graduate will dictate the number of scholarships available year by year. Most programs can also combine financial aid, grants, and academic aid on top of athletic aid.

Different Sports Have Different Odds for a Full Ride Scholarship

The odds for athletic scholarships vary by sport. The figures are complicated by a number of factors such as the number of athletes participating in the sport, the number of colleges that offer the sport, and the number of foreign students competing for a spot. Some sports are "head count sports" which means they only offer full scholarships but the majority of sports can divide their money up. Head count sports include men's and women's basketball, Division I-A football, women's tennis, women's volleyball, and women's gymnastics.

The ratio of athletes to college scholarships helps to clarify the odds of getting an athletic scholarship. This figure is different for men's sports compared to women's, as you can see in the graphs.

Figure 1: Chances of a high school athlete getting a college athletic scholarship

Percentage of high school athletes to scholarships available (2013–14)

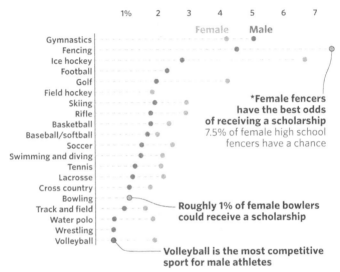

Figure 2: Odds of getting an athletic scholarship for men

NCAA & NAIA schools	Number of high-school athletes	Athletic scholarships	Ratio of high-school athletes to college scholarships
Gymnastics	1,995	101	20:1
Fencing	2,189	99	22:1
Ice hockey	35,393	981	36:1
Football	1,122,024	25,918	43:1
Golf	152,647	2,998	51:1
Skiing - alpine	5,593	107	52:1
Rifle	2,668	47	57:1
Basketball	541,054	9,504	57:1
Baseball	482,629	8,062	60:1
Soccer	417,419	6,152	68:1
Swimming & diving	138,373	1,994	69:1
Tennis	191,004	2,417	79:1
Lacrosse	106,720	1,251	85:1
Cross country	252,547	2,722	93:1
Track & field	653,971	5,930	110:1
Water polo	21,451	126	170:1
Wrestling	269,514	1,530	176:1
Volleyball	52,149	294	177:1

Figure 2: Odds of getting an athletic scholarship for women

NCAA & NAIA schools	Number of high-school athletes	Athletic scholarships	Ratio of high-school athletes to college scholarships
Rowing	4,242	2,080	2:1
Equestrian	1,306	390	3:1
Rugby	322	36	9:1
Fencing	1,774	134	13:1
Ice hockey	9,150	612	15:1
Golf	72,172	3,056	24:1
Gymnastics	19,231	810	24:1
Skiing	4,541	133	34:1
Rifle	1,587	46	35:1
Soccer	374,564	9,266	40:1
Basketball	433,344	10,165	43:1
Lacrosse	81,969	1,779	46:1
Swimming & diving	165,779	3,550	47:1
Tennis	215,737	4,480	48:1
Softball	371,891	7,402	50:1
Volleyball	429,634	8,101	53:1
Field hockey	61,471	1,119	55:1
Water polo	18,899	344	55:1
Cross country	218,121	3,817	57:1
Track & field	545,011	8,536	64:1
Bowling	25,751	275	94:1

Charts from MarketWatch.com website.[9]

Lucy Jenks

Track and Field
Stanford University

From 9th grade to 11th grade, I played on an ECNL soccer team. We had these showcases a few times a year that coaches would watch us play. For those showcases, I would email coaches that I was interested in, and they would come to a game and call me or email my coach if they were interested. By junior year, I was hanging on to soccer because I didn't know if I wanted to fully commit to running, but in the back of my head, I knew that running was going to be my path.

In middle school, I ran the 100 meters for fun. I was always fast at sprinting but I didn't know that I was good at longer distances until freshman year when my high school track coach tested everyone at sprints and distance. He said that I was going to be a good distance runner based on how I tested. Initially I resisted because I had thought of myself as a sprinter and I did not want to run six miles a day. But I liked the girls who ran distance and became friends with them, and it became something fun.

9 Jason Notte. "Here are the best sports for a college scholarship." MarketWatch.com website. 7 November 2018. Retrieved 16 July 2019 from https://www.marketwatch.com/story/these-are-the-sports-your-child-should-play-to-get-a-college-scholarship-2017-05-08

I started running indoor track in freshman year and again in my sophomore year. It wasn't until junior year that I quit my club soccer team and added outdoor track. I trained year-round senior year and ran cross country, indoor and outdoor track. At Nationals, I got fifth place in my event so I made All American.

It helped that I went through the recruiting process for soccer. I had some experience talking to coaches over the phone so I knew what to say to them. When our conversations got closer to committing, I knew that I could run at more academically elite schools than the schools that were interested in me for soccer. Academics were my first and foremost priority. I didn't think that I was going to be a professional runner so I might as well use running to get into the best school possible.

The probability of receiving an athletic scholarship by sport and gender may be a moot point as the high school athlete has already locked down on his or her sport, but multi-sport athletes may find it useful to compare stats.

There are other benefits to playing sports in college besides an athletic scholarship:

- *Love of the Sport*: athletes who fell in love with their sport at a young age will find that there are many options to play sports in college.

- *Instant Social Group*: sports teams of every level provide an instant social group that helps with the transition to college.

- *Healthy Living*: learning about nutrition as part of sports performance, getting regular exercise, and equating food as fuel all help to create a healthy lifestyle that can continue beyond the college experience.

- *Elite Training Opportunities*: student-athletes have access to coaching, athletic facilities, and medical services that come free as part of the college experience, but would be very expensive if paid for privately.

- *Additional Academic and Social-Emotional Support*: additional academic support such as tutors, required study halls, and academic advisors specific to athletes can be part of the support provided by college sports teams. Student-athletes also receive additional social-emotional support resources as part of being on a sports team.

- *Preparation for Life*: training and competing in any sport requires dedication, goal setting, and perseverance: all qualities that help anyone become successful. Additional skills acquired include leadership, time management, and the ability to work collaboratively. All these skills are valued in the workplace and sought out by employers.

- *Student-Athletes are More Successful Academically*[10]: according to the NCAA, college student-athletes graduate at higher rates (currently 82%) than college students in general. This percentage is much higher if football and basketball are excluded.

- *Exposure and Travel Experiences*: elite athletes often are able to travel around the country, and even the world, to compete in events. These travel opportunities can be eye-opening experiences for personal growth.

- *The Discipline of Sport Helps with Overall Organization Skills*: student-athletes have to balance the demands of their sport and academics. These time management skills are valuable life skills.

- *Alumni Network Support*: most colleges have a robust alumni network but alumni who played a sport in college may be particularly generous in helping athletes from that team.

While the probability of receiving a full athletic scholarship is low, there are many benefits to playing sports in college. For any athlete who has set a goal to play sports in college, here is what you need to know to increase your odds of success.

---

[10] "College athletes graduate at record high rates." *NCAA.com* website. Retrieved 14 July 2019 from www.ncaa.org/about/resources/media-center/news/college-athletes-graduate-record-high-rates

Sam Apuzzo
Women's Varsity Lacrosse
Boston College
2018 Tewaaraton Award Winner
Professional Player for New York Fight
US Women's Lacrosse National Team

I played soccer, lacrosse, and basketball as a youth, but lacrosse was my main focus though it didn't start out that way. I started playing lacrosse in 5th grade. A lot of my friends played lacrosse and I really wasn't that interested because I was more of a soccer player at the time. For the most part, I was hesitant to commit to lacrosse. It wasn't something that I thought I would want to do in college.

As I continued playing though, I started to realize that in terms of scholarships, there were more opportunities for lacrosse. I wanted to go to a really competitive school and play at the highest level. There was going to be more opportunity to get a larger scholarship in lacrosse than basketball or soccer for me. Soccer and basketball are really translatable to lacrosse, so it was easy to make that transition.

Being a multi-sport athlete helped me with lacrosse. By the end of the spring and summer season for lacrosse, I would feel overwhelmed and tired from playing so much. I looked forward to taking a break by playing different sports. It helped me from getting burnt out in lacrosse. Both basketball and soccer also kept me in shape, and skills from those sports could be applied to lacrosse. It definitely helped me to become a better lacrosse player by playing other sports.

I started realizing that playing at a Division I level was possible in 7th or 8th grade. I started getting recruited in 9th grade which is when I started doing recruiting trips. It was overwhelming because I was young. I had no idea what to look for in a school or decide where I wanted to be. It all kind of came at once when I was a freshman to feel like I had to officially decide, but I took my time and it wasn't until December of my sophomore year that I made my decision.

I narrowed my list from eight schools to four schools and I took a lot of time to process the pros and cons of each school. I wrote down what I wanted in a school before I began the visits. My parents and I also focused on strong academics, but luckily all four schools were strong in that area.

Location was a big consideration. I am originally from Long Island so I wanted to be close enough so my parents could come to all my games but far enough away that I felt like I was going away to school.

I also wanted to play in a competitive conference so I was looking at schools in the ACC and the Pac 12—programs that I knew were competitive and were always really great teams. I wanted to play at the highest level and be on an elite team that people talk about.

Finally, it came down to team culture and the coach for me. I know that people are told not to go to a school because of a coach because that coach can change. The schools I looked at, the coaches gave me the impression that they were going to be there for the long term.

Team culture was also really important to me. I went on multiple visits to the same place to really get the feel, and I spent a good amount of time with each team. I would picture myself as to whether or not I could fit in with the atmosphere and team dynamic. I was looking for a team that was really close, that didn't have boundaries between each grade because I wanted to be part of something bigger that felt like a family rather than a group of individuals. What drew me to Boston College was that they were really loose and fun but were competitive. They would go at one another but in the best way possible.

My advice to others would be to really take your time. That's what I did. I really thought things through. I didn't just jump at the first offer or the first place that I visited. This is a really big commitment in your life. Really take your time. Write down what you want in a college before you see a school. Understand what you value and take those values to a school to see if they match up.

*To learn more about Sam's professional women's lacrosse league including the game schedule, go to **ProWomensLax.com**.*

What Are Coaches Really Looking For?

College coaches are recruiting prospective student-athletes with a profile that meets the institution's admission standards and requirements. Being a good student will make this process easier for a coach knowing that the PSA is admissible and will be able to handle both the academic and athletic demands. Fundamentally, as an athlete on their team, you are also a student at that college with an expectation that you will graduate.

In two words: academics matter!

How Do They Evaluate Athletes?

Besides your academic and athletic talent, most coaches

pay close attention to your character. To be the right fit for the team, it is important to display the qualities of a good teammate: good sportsmanship, supporting your team and peers through ups and downs, being respectful on and off the field, and accepting your role on the team. With the rise of competitiveness and professionalization in youth sports, many student-athletes are beginning to lose the most important component of athletics: love of the game. Coaches find it harder and harder to recruit athletes who exhibit enthusiasm for their sport. This carries over to enthusiasm both on the bench as well as on the playing field.

What Are Red Flags?

Coaches are observing more than just athletic skills when they attend games and tournaments. The overall behavior of PSAs and their parents on the sidelines does not go unnoticed. Coaches observe a player's demeanor both on and off the field. What is the player's behavior pattern when things are going well? How does the player deal with controversy, such as a bad call by a referee? How does the player behave on the bench when the player feels that he or she should be playing at that moment? Coaches take note of such behavior patterns and are looking for prospects with a positive attitude.

Coaches also notice parental behavior both at athletic events and in the office. One red flag is when a parent dominates the conversation. Coaches notice who is driving the process. Is it the parent or the kid? It's really important for the athlete to take the initiative in the recruiting process and forge a connection with the coach. Make sure that the athlete is the one to respond to emails and calls to college coaches.

John Kennaday
Head Coach Men's Varsity Golf
San Jose State

I'm going to pay very close attention to the relationship between the player and the parent because I'm about to become a pseudo parent to that player. I've seen a tremendous amount of respect and I've seen a tremendous amount of disrespect towards a parent. You can tell when someone has a good relationship; it's in your gut. I've literally seen outbursts of disrespect in my office towards a mother. You pay attention to what's going on between the parents and the kids because that's probably going to be close to what is going to happen with you.

Coaches and Admissions: The Sell to Get You In

In today's admissions process, coaches will have done their due diligence and will, more often than not, know if the prospect is getting admitted or not. In communicating with the coaching staff, it is important to provide them with the requested documentation needed to get an "early admission read." Based on the information provided, the Admissions Office will give the coach an indication if the PSA is an admissible prospect, provided that he or she continues to do the work and perform at that same level in the classroom. If there are admissions questions or concerns, coaches will inform the PSA ahead of time. They will give instructions about what is needed to get admitted based on those details. For example, the PSA may need to retake the SAT test to increase his or her score by 40 points to meet their test requirement. The coach can ONLY support the PSA in this process. The ultimate decision is made in the Admissions Office.

Playing High-Level College Sports is a Full-Time Job

Although the NCAA restricts the number of hours that student-athletes can practice in-season to 20 hours a week or 4 hours per day[11], the reality is that college athletes can spend up to 40 hours a week practicing, according to a 2011 NCAA survey.[12]

---

[11] "Defining Countable Athletically Related Activities." NCAA.com website. Retrieved 3 November 2019 from https://www.ncaa.org/sites/default/files/Charts.pdf

[12] Peter Jacobs. "Here's the Insane Amount of Time College Student-Athletes Spend on Practice." BusinessInsider. com website. 27 January 2015. Retrieved 16 July 2019 from https://www.businessinsider.com/college-student-athletes-spend-40-hours-a-week-practicing-2015-1

On the high side, football players spend 43.3 hours per week, men's basketball 39.2 hours per week, and women's basketball 37.6 hours per week. Still, all other men's and women's Division I sports spent 32-33 hours per week training. The hours athletes can put in vary by level of competition and by sport.

Finding the right balance of academics and athletics is something to consider when evaluating the school that is the right fit for you.

The recruiting process is a marathon, not a sprint. It begins freshman year of high school, or even earlier depending on some sports, and ends when the athlete signs a letter of commitment during his or her senior year of high school.

Much like getting a job, those who are proactive and drive their own process will find success. Athletic skills are important, but this college search process will also call upon your communication, organizational, and time management skills. Let's start with some do's and don'ts of the recruitment process.

Recruiting Don'ts

- Don't have a parent or guardian initiate contact with a coach.

- Don't have a parent or guardian call to praise your skills.

- Don't call and leave a message asking for the coach to call back. You should take the initiative to call back. Coaches are busy people!

- Don't send an email to a coach with the wrong name, the wrong college, or with misspellings.

- Don't mass mail. Customize your communication to the colleges that interest you.

- Don't use a scholarship offer from another college to bargain one school against the other.

- Don't tell a coach the college is at the top of your list if it is not true.

- Don't overestimate your abilities.

- Don't show negative traits in attitude or temperament, etc. Be aware that your body language is also being observed. Exude a positive and confident attitude.

- Don't ask a coach for an official visit, let them offer that to you.

Recruiting Do's

- Do get a binder to track all your recruiting information.

- Do keep a calendar with reminders to keep track of deadlines and dates to make or return calls and emails.

- Do make a list of colleges that have academic and athletic programs that best suit you.

- Do send coaches updated tournament schedules and results.

- Do have a list of credible references.

- Do go to as many college games as possible. Reference those games when talking or communicating to coaches.

- Do ask a reference to make a call on your behalf.

- Do be personable in conversation.

- Do speak positively about other programs, coaches, and players.

- Do make yourself known. One email is not going to do it.

- Do stay on top of your academics. It shows your work habits, time management, and commitment to achievement. These are all characteristics that colleges look for.

- Do send thank-you notes (the old-fashioned kind that you mail with a postage stamp) when a coach has taken time to talk or meet with you.

- Do read up on the college prior to a visit with a coach. Be prepared to answer questions about the institution that are non-athletic related.

- Do prepare three to four questions about the institution and coaching program.

- Do display positive energy throughout a campus visit.

The timeline for the recruiting process begins in freshman year in high school. Let's get started!

Kelly Doton
Head Coach Women's Field Hockey
ACC Coach of the Year
NCAA Final Four 2019
US Field Hockey Coach
Boston College

The Do's

- Research/visit as many schools as you can in order to figure out what you like and don't like in the school (size/location/competition level etc.).

- Be open and honest with the coaching staff. If you aren't interested in a school, it's okay to tell the coaching staff. They need to hear that.

- Make a Pros/Cons list of the universities you have visited and make it detailed.

- Ask questions. We don't know what you don't know.

- Enjoy the process! It may seem stressful, and create anxiety, but make it as enjoyable as possible.

- Do ask how the financial aid process works.

The Don'ts

- Don't narrow your school choices too early. You may find a university you love that was never on your list.

- Don't visit a school that doesn't have a major you want. It will make it worse in the long run.

- Don't let your parents handle the conversations with the coaches. We want to hear from you.

- Don't let your social media posts be a red flag.

- Don't be rushed into a decision because of a deadline. Make your decision based on your research and process.

THE RECRUITING TIMELINE: EARLY DECISION VERSUS REGULAR ADMISSIONS

The different divisions of colleges all have a slightly different recruiting timeline. You first want to find out if an institution has an early decision process or if the admissions is based on rolling admissions.

There are two ways to apply early to colleges. Early Action (EA) is nonbinding in that students receive an early response from the college but are not committed to attend there. They can wait to hear from all the colleges that they applied to and then decide where they want to go by the normal reply date of May 1st. Early Decision (ED) is a binding agreement in which you agree to attend that college should they offer you admission. Upon acceptance, you agree to withdraw applications from all other colleges. Early Decision applications are usually due in early or mid-November. You can only apply to ONE college Early Decision. Some colleges have two periods of Early Decision: ED 1 and ED 2. ED 2 is similar to ED 1 in that the decision is binding. ED 2 deadlines are typically around January 1st – similar to Regular Decision deadlines – and offers a second chance to choose a school to commit to if the student has been rejected from his or her ED 1 choice.

Early Action has the same early application deadline of beginning or mid-November. Early Action is non-binding; the student does not have to commit to that college until the normal decision date of May 1st which allows the student to make their decision based on responses from other colleges.

Regular Decision admissions tend to have an application due date in early January with a decision to students between March and April.

"Rolling Decision admissions" means that the college allows students to apply any time within a large window. This means that the admissions process continues deep into the summer period, even into August for some institutions. Some colleges do have firm deadlines when applications are due. You can apply to as many schools as you like, as there is no limit! This would allow you to compare schools before you make a final decision on your school of choice.

The majority of Division I colleges will fill their recruiting class by early fall of that class's senior year, or earlier, depending on the college. This means that if you are a Division I athlete, you have already visited the college, sat down with the coach, and know where you stand on their recruiting list by your first day of class senior year.

Division II colleges are typically the next to finish up their recruiting classes. Most schools will still recruit throughout the year, even during the summer leading up to pre-season in August. Most colleges have a rolling admissions process and remain very flexible when it comes to athletics.

The recruiting process in Division I and II will be impacted and influenced by the financial process and available resources. The process that potentially involves an athletic scholarship versus no scholarship can alter the timeline for the PSA and the decision-making process. Coaches will often set firm deadlines when they expect a commitment from the PSA regarding the scholarship offer.

Division III colleges also look to finish their recruitment through the fall semester. The higher the academic level, the earlier coaches finalize their rosters. Other schools have a rolling admissions process and remain very flexible when it comes to athletics.

NAIA and Junior Colleges have the most flexibility with regard to the admissions deadlines. Their recruiting typically continues into the winter and spring of a student-athlete's senior year of high school.

If you are not on track with these timelines, do not panic. These are general guidelines and every college has a different situation. Just bear in mind that the higher the academic standards of an institution, the earlier the timeline for admissions deadlines.

The next sections will break down the action steps that athletes need to take during their freshman, sophomore, junior, and senior years of high school.

Tips:

- Coaches continue to follow your progress and development in school and on the field.

- Standouts are proactive, it's never too early for YOU to write a letter or make a call to Division III coaches since the rules are much more flexible and they CAN respond to a phone call.

- DIII and NAIA coaches can contact you at any time.

- It is important for you to be familiar with the school both athletically and academically. If you are considering a NAIA program, register with the NAIA Eligibility Center.

- Contact coaches at least once a month starting in junior year.

- Respond to EVERY coach, even if you are not interested in the school.

HIGH SCHOOL FRESHMAN YEAR

Selecting Colleges: Creating an Initial List

The first draft of a college list can be as long or as short as the athlete wants it to be. The goal is just to create a list on paper. The initial list of colleges might pull from your experiences from watching a college team, attending a sports camp, or playing at a college's sports facility.

This initial list is the first step in defining what kind of experience the athlete is seeking. Things to consider include location, size of school, enrollment, and academic requirements. Once a few of the colleges are identified, researched, and confirmed as a good fit, it can be used as a reference point to branch out to similar schools in other geographic areas.

A college is a good fit if it meets your definition of what you are looking for. The criteria will be personal in terms of priority but it will probably include aspects such as academic programs, size, location, and cost.

Your initial list should include a range of schools in terms of selectivity with "reach," "target" and "likely" colleges. Don't assume that athletic skill means that the coach can make an exception for lower grades and standardized test scores outside the school's median range.

When looking at schools, try to find a campus that you can relate to and which feels comfortable: a campus where you can see yourself attending for four to five years. Look for a school that meets your academic needs and an athletic program where you feel wanted and believe that you can succeed. Be honest with yourself about where you might fit in academically and athletically, asking yourself if this institution provides the right balance academically, athletically, and socially.

Sarah Dacey

Head Coach Women's Soccer

Barry University

2018 and 2019 Conference Coach of the Year

3 Time National Champion at UNC in Soccer

2 Time NCAA Final Four at UNC in Lacrosse

Do your research.

Figure out what kind of school will fit you best. Get a feel for the campus, big or small, the academic reputation, majors available, campus living, dining hall, social life, etc. It's not always just about the athletics. Decide on a school based on if you weren't to play a sport ... would it fulfill you and make you happy to go there? Education is the priority!

Also, make sure you do get a feel for the current team, coaching staff, facilities, team culture, how successful the team has been in recent years, number of players who play your position etc. This will give you a better understanding of what you are looking for and the impact you could have on a program.

Size Matters

In thinking about the size of a college, start with the size of your high school, specifically the number of students in your grade. How does your current class size feel to you? Do you want to go smaller, larger, or stay the same? This can point you in the direction of the size of the school.

A college is a smaller institution that focuses on undergraduate education. A university offers both undergraduate and graduate degrees. Colleges can vary in size from a few thousand students to tens of thousands. But even very large universities can be segmented for a "college within a college" feeling. Not sure? No problem. Visit schools of different sizes to get a sense of what feels comfortable to you. You might be surprised!

Geography

Going to college is a chance to explore the world and try out a new geographic area that perhaps you have never been to before. Start with where you live. Is it rural, suburban, or urban? Do you have strong feelings of wanting to live in a similar setting or want to try something drastically different? How far away do you want to go from home? One hour? Across the country? Near a beach? In a college town? In a city? What is your ideal weather? Where is the nearest city and airport? How long is will it take from door to door?

Visiting colleges will give you a chance to see different types of environments and decide where you want to live for the next four years.

Academics

When it comes to academics, you don't necessarily need to decide now what you want to major in but perhaps you already know what your academic areas of interest are. College is also a great place to explore different areas of study. It's important to keep an open mind.

Questions to consider might be about keeping your options open. How easy is it to double major or add a minor? Are there special programs that you might be interested in such as conservatory, fine arts, nursing, ROTC, business, or teaching?

You might also want to consider what the teaching environment is like. What courses are required and is there a distribution requirement? Are academic support services provided?

For athletes seeking a rigorous academic experience, inquire about opportunities beyond the classroom experience. Do professors do research? How easy is it for undergraduates to get research opportunities? Does the college offer an honors program? Are there travel abroad programs both during the school year and summer?

Steph McCaffrey

Varsity Women's Soccer
Boston College
Played Professionally for the Boston Breakers and Chicago Red Stars
U.S. Women's National Soccer Team Member

The number one factor for me in choosing a college was the soccer program. I was looking at how good they were and how willing they were to invest in me. I looked for a track record of developing players that were like me. Although I was being recruited by top schools like Stanford and UNC, I thought that I was pretty raw. Some programs like Boston College and UVA appeared more willing to develop players during their freshman year.

I noticed at Boston College that there were a lot of forwards who coach kept out of the starting line-up freshman year, but then put them into the starting line-up for the next three years. Even though it was frustrating not starting as a freshman, coach knew what would be best for me in the long run. It made me more driven. It allowed me to work on things that I needed to improve on in training for a game environment. Instead of a sophomore slump, it prepared me for a sophomore break out season.

I also thought analytically about the evaluation that

coaches gave me as a player on what I should work on. I was intentional about asking coaches specifically about what plans, drills, or strategies they had for developing me.

The second thing was the quality of life that I would have at the university, specifically the team culture and how close that was to home. When I was being recruited, I was young – fifteen and sixteen years old – and going far away wasn't going to make me happy. That being said, if the team culture was going to provide a family environment, I would have considered going further away. Boston College gave me the best of both worlds.

Finally, I looked at academics. I wanted an undergraduate business program. It was looking like I would be able to play professionally after school. I wanted to close the gap so that when I'm in the position that I am in now, getting an M.B.A. at Wharton, I wouldn't be in over my head.

I give a lot of credit to Alison Foley and the coaching staff for developing me to help me reach my goals of playing professionally and for the U.S. National Team.

If you are undecided in terms of your future major, you might want to consider colleges that are strong in both liberal arts and the sciences. These institutions won't allow you to choose a major until after your freshman year to encourage you to explore and be open-minded toward your course selection as a freshman.

Social

Your college experience will be more than sports and academics. It will also be the network of new friends that you make and the experiences you have outside the classroom. What is important to you when you are not in class or playing your sport?

Where you live during your time in college is something to consider. Do you want to live on campus for all four years of college? What percent of students live on campus? What types of housing options are available (learning communities, Greek, single sex living, substance free, athletic dorm)?

You might also want to consider who your classmates will be. What is your ideal ethnic/diversity mix, gender diversity ratio, and geographic distribution? Would you consider single-sex school or a Historically Black College (HBC)? If there is a Greek system, what percentage of students participate? Does this college have a religious affiliation and how does that impact class requirements? What is the atmosphere of the college: conservative/liberal, artsy, LGBTQ+ friendly, strong Greek life, school spirited, or religious?

Admissions Selectivity

Most colleges will give a GPA and SAT/ACT score range for their accepted students. While students do get accepted outside of this range, it gives parameters for what is "ball park".

What is the average GPA and standardized test scores for the college? How does this fit into your balanced list of colleges in terms of "reach," "target," and "likely?" You will want to track this information for each of the schools on your college list.

A growing trend in college admissions is "test optional" which means that the school does not require SAT or ACT scores from applicants in order to be considered for admission. More than 1000 colleges are currently "test optional" including many academically competitive schools like University of Chicago and Bucknell University who eliminated standardized tests recently. (Test optional often does not apply for a PSA since they still have to submit standardized test scores for the NCAA eligibility center, so there CAN be a difference in the admissions process for regular students versus PSAs.)

Financial

Who is paying the bill? Are you seeking financial aid? Does the institution have merit scholarships? Paid internships? Athletic scholarships? All of the above?

How much does college cost?

All colleges list the cost of tuition, room and board on their website. Check to see if there is in-state versus out-of-state tuition costs.

Public colleges can cost half the amount of private colleges, but there is a wide range of costs between public colleges. Canadian colleges are another option, and they can also cost half the amount of private American colleges.

In your research notes, you might want to track the cost of each college on your list as it pertains to you.

When it comes to financial aid, there are many factors to consider that won't be clear until you receive a financial aid package. Still, you can research and track some useful information about the colleges' financial aid philosophies.

Some questions to consider are what percentage of a financial aid package is composed of loans versus grants? Is there a household income threshold that guarantees 100% financial aid? Are there merit-based scholarships? These answers can produce very different outcomes when it comes to financing a college education.

For example, getting 100% financial aid in the form of grants (not loans) from a more expensive private college could be more affordable than taking out loans to pay for a public university where tuition is half the cost of a private college.

Though you will want to know the cost of college, you will need to analyze each financial aid and athletic scholarship offer to really understand what it will actually cost you and your family.

You also have to factor in additional expenses such as books, travel to home, personal expenses, and supplies for a particular major, such as art.

For information on costs, here are a few websites:

Tuition Tracker: **www.tuitiontracker.org**

College Results: **www.collegeresults.org/default.aspx**

College Data: **www.collegedata.com**

Athletics

As you begin your college search, start to define what kind of athletic program is the right 'fit' for you. For each athlete, this is, perhaps, a different and personal decision. For example, are there colleges that you might be interested in as a recruit versus some that you might consider as a walk-on?

Each athlete might ask him or herself:

- Would I improve here?

- Would I choose this college if I wasn't on the team?

- Would I choose this college if there is a different coach?

- Would I be happy if I don't get a lot of playing time?
- Is this a school that fits me academically and athletically?
- What kind of team culture am I looking for?

Make a list of your top priorities in a college. Take that list with you for each college visit and keep track of what the school has and doesn't have. Once the list exists, it's helpful to pose some questions in order to start analyzing these opportunities.

One important point to remember: the college recruiting process is a two-way street. Every athlete should realize that coaches want to make sure that you are a good fit for their program while they evaluate you. You must do the same thing as well. This is a journey to explore and discover what might be the most important factors TO YOU of where to go after high school.

Peter Kim
Head Coach Women's Soccer
Assistant Coach Men's and Women's Track and Field
Middlebury College

Do your research. Visit campus, connect with current and former students, and ask the hard questions. Go beyond the standard list of questions that everyone asks, and instead ask ones that will give you the information you need to make an educated decision. Compare the answers you get with what you've observed during your visits. Important note: remember that this is your job, not your parents'! Mom and Dad are important resources and sounding boards, but the work and all of the contact with coaches should come from you.

Coaching Staff

As you analyze college athletic programs, you are also considering college coaches and their coaching style. You might want to think about the various coaching styles that you have experienced as an athlete to figure out if there is a certain coaching style that you thrive under. And is there a style that has not worked for you? Can you describe the ideal coaching style you are seeking?

In many programs, the assistant coaches do most of the initial work. They identify and communicate with the PSAs. They carry out the philosophy of the program and look to identify prospects that fit their style of play or other requirements for their team. At the Division I level, the head coach may evaluate your performance in the process but you may not have much interaction until the later stages when you have become a more serious candidate who they are interested in. Besides your communication with the assistants, you want to ask players to define the coaching style of their program. You want to make sure that the players experience the same coaching style explained by the staff.

There is always turnover in athletics in both assistant and head coaching positions. Evaluate colleges and athletic programs with and without the head coach. Is this a school you would still want to attend even if the head coach is no longer there?

Greg DiCenzo
Head Coach Baseball
College of the Holy Cross

The recruiting process can be burdensome and overwhelming, to say the least. The pressure of finding the best school, with the best coaches and the best program is a never-ending game of hide-and-seek. So ... stop searching for the BEST. Work diligently in finding the RIGHT fit for you and your family. Do not simply lust over the logo on the front of the jersey, but rather, fall in love with the coach and teammates wearing them. Search tirelessly to find a coach who will care more about who you are as a person than what you can do on the field of play. It may (and should!) take significant time and energy to ask the pointed questions that will ultimately lead you to the RIGHT fit. Such questions may steer you away from a set location that you had only pursued, or perhaps a level of competition (Division I, II, or III) that you had not explored. Keep your options open, be persistent, and at the end of the day ... ENJOY THE PROCESS! This should be a fun experience, and if pursued appropriately, will provide you with the necessary tools to answer the most important question, once your athletic career has ended ... "what's next?"

Let the Research Begin!

After you create your list of colleges, it's time to research! Do you like sleuthing on social media? Start with your list of colleges and connect to all the colleges' social media, and read their websites.

Your list is just getting started. Check college resource books, meet with your high school's college and/or guidance counselor, and utilize resources that your school might offer, like software for American college and career readiness such as Naviance.

There are many college resource books that more or less have the same information. Here are some of the recommended guides that you can find at your library:

- Fiske Guide to Colleges
- Petersen's Four-Year Colleges

- The Big Book of Colleges
- The Best 381 Colleges
- The Insider's Guide to the Colleges
- Find the Best Colleges for You
- The College Board College Handbook
- Colleges that Change Lives
- The Hidden Ivies: 63 of America's Top Liberal Arts Colleges and Universities

This is also the time to revise, edit, and expand your college list as you hone in on the factors that are important to you.

Sarah Dacey
Head Coach Women's Soccer
Barry University

Do have a good understanding of what level will fit you best?

Not everyone is a Division I athlete and not every player will be guaranteed playing time. There are many benefits to playing in all divisions. Being a part of a team, making great friends, and having life long memories is the ultimate goal.

Create a Tracking System

It's going to be important to create a system to track and organize your research and communications with college coaches. Colleges, coaches, and programs will start to blur together. Whether it's a binder with a tab for each college, a spreadsheet, or a journal, keep track of your research and note all communication, including what was sent out, the date, and the nature of the response. This tracking system will also include your impressions as you interact with the coaching staff, attend their college camps and games, and meet players on the team.

Figure 4: Example of a spreadsheet:

	College	City	State	League	Coach	Ast Coach	Ast Coach	Visited
CT	Sacred Heart	Fairfield	CT	Northeast Conference	Matt Meros	Scott McBride	Paulo DeOliveira	Yes
	Quinnipiac	Hamden	CT	Metro Atlantic Athletic Conference	Dave Clarke	Steve Coxen	Sara Tompkins	Yes
	Hartford	West Hartford	CT	America East	John Natale	Todd Sadler		
	Fairfield	Fairfield	CT	Metro Atlantic Athletic Conference	David Barrett	Sydney Stoll		Yes
MA	Holy Cross	Worcester	MA	Patriot League	Casey Brown	Caitlin Pickul		Yes
	UMASS	Amherst	MA	Atlantic 10	Jason Dowiak	Marsha Harper	Sam Mithcell	Yes
	BU	Boston	MA	Patriot League	Nancy Feldman	Kelly Lawrence	Tori Christ	No
NH	UNH	Durham	NH	America East	Steve Welham	Amanda Bowes		
NY	Siena	Loudonville	NY	Metro Atlantic Athletic Conference	Steve Karbowski	Dara Battistoni	Todd Bradshaw	
	Colgate	Hamilton	NY	Patriot League	Kathy Brown	Alyssa Manoogian	Jenna Gibney	
	Iona	New Rochelle	NY	Metro Atlantic Athletic Conference				
RI	URI	South Kingston	RI	Atlantic 10	Megan Jesse	James Thorpe	Jenna Kalwai	Yes
	Bryant	Smithfield	RI	Northeast Conference	Andy Biggs	Ashley Heidelberger		Yes
	Brown	Providence	RI	Ivy	Kia McNeil	Raleigh DeRose	Matt Mones	No
VT	UVM	Burlington	VT	America East	Kristi Huizenga	Lauren Cootware (Bernard)		Yes
PA	Duquesne	Madison	PA	A10	Al Alvine	Erica Marshall		Yes

Figure 5: Example of a spreadsheet:

ID Camp Attn	Notes							
	general email invites to camps with direct correspondence							
	general email invites to camps with direct correspondence							
	multiple email interactions from TS....watched Grace play in Spring-19 game (not a good game), silent since that game							
	general email invites to camps with direct correspondence (seen Grace play in Tournaments)							
11/17/19	Attended camp...email correspondence with CP (seen Grace play in Tournaments)							
3/30/19	Attended camp...phone conversation JD							
	Was emailed invite to summer camp in response to "thank you email" for attending Top 100							
	general email invites to camps with direct correspondence							
	general email invites to camps... no direct correspondence							
	N/A							
	N/A							
4/20/19	Attended camp and have had phone call with JT (seen Grace play in tournaments)							
1/6/19 & 4/7/2018	Attended 2 camps. AH emailed Brendan to have Grace call her after August-18 Camp....we left AH a VM. Seems a bit quieter after the Jan-19 camp (attended games ;							
	Was emailed invite to summer camp in response to "thank you email" for attending Top							
2/9/19	Attended Exact Camp in 2018 and had LB as coach. Attended UVM camp in Feb-19...LB provided some feedback to AF							
2/23/19	Attended camp...was invited from coach who attended SSS/Aztec Showcase in Jan-19...that coach has now left Duquesne							

Keep a Recruiting Calendar

Consider using an online or paper calendar to keep track of important dates such as deadlines for applications, calls to coaches, and school visits. Set up reminders one or two days before each deadline to ensure that you don't miss anything important.

Play at the Highest Level Possible

Playing on the most competitive team and in the most competitive environment will not only help you get better, but expose you to coaches who look for players they think can compete at their institution's level. In general, it is important to play on a team that attends tournaments and events where college coaches attend to recruit.

Keep a Record of Your Athletic Achievements

It's time to start an athletic resume that will include both team and individual achievements. This is a work in progress so just document and note dates, locations, teams, as well as achievements. Create a document to track all this information. It will be used to create your athletic resume. Any achievements from 9th grade forward should be included.

Academics are Very Important

Juggling academics with sports is a challenge for all student-athletes both in high school and college. Your ability to perform both in the classroom and on the sports field in high school is a proxy for how you will do in college. Keep your grades up. Realize that academics are going to be an important component of how desirable a recruit you are. As a freshman in high school, there is a world of possibilities. Admissions staff will look at your academic performance from the day you enter 9th grade.

Social Media

Consider your social media footprint to be public and accessible, even if it is set to private. Be mindful of what you are posting; comments and posts need to be respectful and professional. How you conduct yourself on social media is just as important as how you conduct yourself at school or athletic events.

Coaches must follow NCAA rules in terms of contact with PSAs and that includes communication using social media. For most Division I sports, coaches can communicate with athletes starting on June 15 after sophomore year. Prior to that, the NCAA stipulates that "If a coach becomes aware that a recruit has elected to receive direct messages as text messages on a mobile device, the coach must cease communicating with the recruit through the social networking site. All other electronically transmitted correspondence including, but not limited to, text messaging, instant messenger, chat rooms, message boards, or walls within social networking websites remain impermissible."

ID Camps

Identification camps are a great way to be seen and evaluated. ID camps and clinics are mainly an opportunity for the PSA to perform in front of college coaches on the institution's campus. They want to see if you are the type of athlete that they can see as a fit for their program. You may not always get an evaluation given that it is a snapshot performance. The majority of sports cannot comment on your play or potential as a recruit at their school. They need to follow the NCAA rules that prohibit them from speaking about recruiting you until June 15th after your sophomore year. **Be aware of the communication rules for sports** as silence is often misunderstood for lack of interest. The coaches are likely just following the rules.

Learn about the Governing Bodies: NCAA, NAIA, NJCAA, and NCCAA

Familiarize yourself with the various associations that govern collegiate sports. Start your research by learning about the NCAA eligibility center academic requirements and amateur status: **https://web3.ncaa.org/ecwr3/**

This PDF from NCAA answers questions for student-athletes and parents navigating the initial eligibility process: **www.ncaapublications.com/productdownloads/CBSA19.pdf**

Even if you don't have any NCAA Division I or II colleges on your list, it's still important to understand the sports recruiting landscape.

NCAA Guidelines

The National Collegiate Athletic Association (NCAA) is an organization that regulates student athletes from more than 1,200 North American institutions and conferences. Students who plan to compete in athletics at the college level need to meet certain eligibility requirements. The Eligibility Center is the organization within the NCAA that determines the academic eligibility and amateur status for all NCAA DI and DII athletes. Athletes who have not met the NCAA eligibility requirements are not allowed to participate in college sports at these schools.

For information go to:
https://web1.ncaa.org/eligibilitycenter/common

NCAA Initial-Eligibility Clearinghouse

If your college list includes NCAA Division I or II schools, you will need to register with the NCAA Eligibility Center the summer before your junior year of high school. As a freshman in high school, you don't need to register yet, but just familiarize yourself with the NCAA eligibility requirements.

The NCAA Divisions: Division I, II, and III

Division I

More than 350 colleges and universities with more than 6,000 athletic teams comprise the roughly 170,000 student-athletes in NCAA Division I. The Division I conferences include the SEC, Big 10, Pac 12 and ACC. Division I has the largest student bodies and gives out the most athletic scholarships.

The Ivy League is also Division I but these colleges do not give out athletic scholarships. Colleges that comprise the Ivy League are Brown, Cornell, Dartmouth, Harvard, the University of Pennsylvania, Princeton, and Yale.

For a list of member schools/sports: **https://web3.ncaa.org/ecwr3/**

Recruiting Rules for the Majority of Division I Olympic Sports

Football has very different windows of time in the recruiting process. For example, there are no restrictions on when coaches can extend verbal offers to recruits. Starting from September 1st of junior year, football recruits can receive private communication including emails, texts, recruiting materials, text, and direct messages. Football recruits can take ONE official visit starting from April 1st to the last Wednesday in June but it may not be in conjunction with a camp or clinic. Beginning from April 15th to May 31st of their junior year, coaches can call the football recruits once. Additional calls can be made from September 1st of the recruits' senior year. Recruits can take five official visits starting from September 1st of their senior year.

In men's basketball, coaches can call, email, text, and direct message with recruits. At the start of their junior year coaches can conduct an off-campus meeting at the recruit's school or residence. Starting from January 1st of their junior year, they can take up to five official visits.

For women's basketball, coaches can start sending emails, texts, and coaches can make an unlimited number of phone calls starting from September 1st of the recruit's junior year. On March 1st of the recruit's junior year, coaches are allowed to conduct off-campus visits at the recruits' school or residence. On the Thursday after the NCAA Women's Final

Four, juniors are allowed to start their five official visits.

In men's ice hockey, coaches are allowed to begin calling, texting, emailing, and direct messaging recruits on January 1st of their sophomore year. They can also make unofficial visits at this time. Starting from June 15th after their sophomore year, coaches can make off-campus contact with recruits. Starting August 1st before their junior year, ice hockey recruits can start taking their five official visits.

In women's ice hockey, coaches can start calling, texting, emailing and direct messaging on June 15th after their sophomore year. Recruits can start their five official visits on August 1st before their junior year. They do not have the January 1st sophomore year exception.

In men's and women's lacrosse, everything happens on September 1st of the recruits' junior year. Coaches can call, text, email and direct message starting on this day. This is the first date recruits can go on an unofficial or official visit. Coaches are also allowed to conduct off-campus meetings at the school or residence of the recruit.

Women's softball is the same as lacrosse with the exception that they cannot conduct an off-campus visit at the recruits' school or residence until July 1st before the recruits' junior year.

Below are the rules for all other Division I Sports

Freshman and Sophomore Year

Recruiting Material: You may receive brochures for camps and questionnaires.

Telephone Calls: Not allowed.

Unofficial Visits: Unlimited but no contact with the coaches.

Official Visits: Not allowed.

Off Campus Contact: Not allowed.

Junior Year

Recruiting Material: You may begin to receive recruiting materials and information from the coach on June 15th after sophomore year.

Telephone Calls: You may make unlimited calls to the coach at your own expense starting from June 15th after sophomore year.

Unofficial Visits: Unlimited

Official Visits: August 1st of junior year for Division I and II (limited to five). Division III starts on January 15th and unlimited visits.

Off Campus Contact: Not allowed.

Senior Year

Recruiting Material: You may receive recruiting material and information from the coach

Telephone Calls: You may make unlimited calls to the coach at your own expense; you can receive one call per week in Division I and II.

Unofficial Visits: Unlimited.

Official Visits: You may begin official visits on August 1st of your junior year; you get one per college and a maximum of five visits to DI and DII. DIII has unlimited visits starting on January 15th of junior year.

Division II

There are more than 300 Division II schools, and they also give out athletic scholarships. Division II schools are smaller in student population than Division I schools. Division II schools award fewer athletic scholarships than Division I colleges, and often award partial athletic scholarships.

For a list of member schools:
http://web1.ncaa.org/memberLinks/links.jsp?div=2

Recruiting Rules for Division II (for all sports)

Freshman and Sophomore Year

Recruiting Material: You may receive brochures for camps and questionnaires only.

Telephone Calls: Not allowed until June 15th after sophomore year.

Unofficial Visits: Athletes can make unofficial visits anytime.

Official Visits: Not allowed.

Off Campus Contact: Not allowed.

Junior Year

Recruiting Material: You may receive recruiting material and information from the coach starting on June 15th after sophomore year.

Telephone Calls: The college coach can call an unlimited number of times starting on June 15th prior to junior year.

Unofficial Visits: Athletes can take unofficial visits at any time.

Official Visits: Not allowed until June 15th after your sophomore year.

Off Campus Contact: Coaches can conduct off-campus communication with athletes and or their family starting on June 15th after the athlete's sophomore year.

Senior Year

Recruiting Material: You can receive recruiting material and information from the coach.

Telephone Calls: The college coach can call you an unlimited number of times starting on June 15th after sophomore year.

Unofficial Visits: Unlimited.

Official Visits: You can begin official visits starting on June 15th after your sophomore year.

Off Campus Contact: After June 15th of sophomore year, college coaches may begin to conduct off-campus communications with athletes and their parents.

Division III

The largest NCAA division is Division III with more than 444 institutions and more than 170,000 student-athletes.

Division III colleges do not give out athletic scholarships; however, athletes can get need-based or academic financial aid.

Division III athletic programs generally have shorter practice hours and less travel for games.

For a list of member schools:
http://web1.ncaa.org/memberLinks/links.jsp?div=3

Recruiting Rules for Division III (for all sports)

For All Years of High School

Recruiting Material: You can receive recruiting material and information from the coach at any time.

Telephone Calls: The college coach can call or contact you digitally an unlimited number of times.

Unofficial Visits: Unlimited.

Official Visits: You can start official visits after January 1st of your junior year.

Off Campus Contact: After the athlete's sophomore year, college coaches may begin to conduct off-campus communications with athletes and their parents.

For a list of member schools:
www.ncaa.org/about/division-iii-schools

Steph McCaffrey
Varsity Women's Soccer
Boston College
Played Professionally for the Boston Breakers and Chicago Red Stars
U.S. Women's National Soccer Team Member

In terms of making a decision of where to play in college, take as much time as you can. For me, having to commit to a college as a fifteen-year-old was not appropriate or fair. I would advise that if coaches are pressing you to give an answer by your sophomore year, that is a sign that this might not be the best place for you. I think that the coach who really cares about you would understand that, given the age range that we are expecting kids to make life changing decisions, giving you as much flexibility as possible is a clear indication of what it will be like to play for that coach.

The NAIA

The National Association of Intercollegiate Athletics (NAIA) is a college athletics association for small colleges and universities in North America. The NAIA has different eligibility requirements for student-athletes.

Incoming freshmen must meet **two of the three** following requirements:

1. Have a minimum score of 16 on the ACT or 860 on the SAT

2. Achieve an overall high school GPA of at least 2.0 on a 4.0 scale

3. Graduate in the top half of their high school class

Athletes who must register with the NAIA include:

- High school seniors, both U.S. and international
- Home schooled and GED students
- Current NAIA students who will be playing sports for the first time at an NAIA school
- Transfers from two-year colleges
- Transfers from four-year colleges

If you are registered with the NCAA but plan to play for an NAIA school, you must register with the NAIA. The NCAA and NAIA are two separate governing bodies with different sets of rules and certification processes.

If you have questions about NAIA eligibility, contact them from Monday through Friday, from 8:30am to 5pm CT at the NAIA Eligibility Center phone: 1-816-595-8300 or email at **ECinfo@naia.org** (U.S. students); **ECinternational@naia.org** (international students).

For a list of member schools: **www.naia.org/schools/index**

For rules on financial aid: **www.naia.org/membership/2017-18/releases/financial-aid**

For rules on campus visits: **www.naia.org/legislative/recruitment** and **www.naia.org/legislative/2016-17/releases/20161011ymuph**

The NJCAA

The National Junior College Athletic Association (NJCAA) is the governing body of intercollegiate athletics for two-year colleges.

For information on schools and eligibility requirements go to: **www.njcaa.org/**

For a list of member schools by gender and sport: **https://stats.njcaa.org/member_colleges/college-directory**

The NCCAA

The National Christian College Athletic Association is an association of Christian universities, colleges and Bible colleges in the United States and Canada.

For information on schools and eligibility requirements go to: **www.thenccaa.org**

For a list of member schools by region: **www.thenccaa.org/ sports/2017/6/14/Member_Schools_17-18.aspx**

Homeschooled Athletes

Homeschooled students who want to play DI or DII college sports must register with the clearinghouse and meet the same requirements as all other students.

The NCAA has a toolkit for homeschooled athletes: **http:// fs.ncaa.org/Docs/eligibility_center/Student_Resources/ Home_School_Toolkit_for_Public.pdf**

The NCAA also has resource for homeschool education history: **http://fs.ncaa.org/Docs/eligibility_center/ Tutorials/2016_How_to_Fill_Out_Home_School_ Education_History_20161101.pdf**

The Rules for College Coach Communication

The rules have changed for many Division I coaches in most sports as to when they are allowed to contact a high school athlete, and this is one of the most confusing aspects of the college recruitment process.

Coach contact depends on the sport, age, division level, and type of communication. Some of these items pertain to NCAA schools only. The governing organizations meet on a regular basis and can change the rules. It's always best to check with the umbrella organization to verify recruitment rules.

For example, the NCAA recently instated a new set of rules for many Division I sports, including timeframes for which college coaches can contact athletes. However, football, women's and men's basketball, softball, baseball and women's and men's lacrosse were exempted from these new rules. Men's ice hockey has also changed their rules.

Familiarize yourself with the NCAA recruiting rules of when college coaches can contact high school athletes here: **www. ncsasports.org/ncaa-eligibility-center/recruiting-rules**

It's important to realize that for most high school freshmen or sophomores, NCAA Division I and II college coaches CAN NOT call or write to you. This includes all forms of communication including emails, texts, and phone calls. Division III coaches do not have these communication restrictions.

The list of college programs that you identified during your freshman year will likely change over time as new schools will be added and others deleted. The list of interested schools is likely to change due to the interest that you receive from colleges, based on your academic achievements, standardized test results, and levels of communication, especially after June 15th after your sophomore year.

Division I college coaches can't answer your phone calls or call you until June 15th after your sophomore year. If you wish to visit a campus you can, but you can't meet with the coach or coaching staff.

You can take as many unofficial campus visits as you wish.

Division II and III and NAIA unofficial visits are unlimited and can take place at any time. Unofficial visits for Division I where you meet with the coaching staff or any athletic representative of the school, cannot take place until August 1st of junior year. From that date, unofficial visits to D1 colleges are also unlimited. The sports for which this is an exception are football, baseball, softball, men's and women's lacrosse and women's basketball.

How about "official" visits? Official visits, which are limited to five, are paid for by the school. The dates of when official visits can occur vary by sport and range from August 1st prior to junior year to January 1st of junior year."

Peter Kim
Head Coach Women's Soccer
Assistant Coach Men's and Women's Track and Field
Middlebury College

Don't fall for sales pitches. Coaches may want you to come to their school to help them win games. While many coaches will be honest with you, they are still speaking to you from the vantage point of filling their needs for the team. Your decision-making process should be about satisfying your needs, not anyone else's!

What is the Role of My High School and Club Coach?

College coaches may contact your high school and club team coach to express interest in an athlete and to learn more about that person. Your high school and/or club team coach will play a key role in communicating to college coaches on your behalf.

College Coach Questionnaire

All college programs provide the opportunity for a PSA to complete an athletic questionnaire on the sport's website. This is an opportunity for you to provide personal and specific athletic related information.

Lucy Jenks
Track and Field
Stanford University

My advice would be to reach out to schools. I know that with soccer, I didn't always feel like I was good enough.

I wavered about whether or not I should email certain colleges, but the worst that can happen is that they don't respond or they say no.

I remember feeling uncertain about reaching out to Stanford for running. That was before Nationals. But they got back to me and that was when the dialogue started.

I would say to shoot your shot. Be aggressive about emailing and calling the coaches. Show them that you are interested. Also try not to make your decision under pressure. Take your time and really think it through.

Why You Should Respond to Every Coach:

- As an underclassman, you might be receiving general admissions information. Responding will keep your options open!

- You may change your mind as you research a college and get to know the coaching staff and players. Your initial impression of a perfect college or program may also change over time.

- Learning to effectively communicate with coaches takes time and practice. Practice these skills by talking and emailing to coaches who are lower on your list.

- As you learn about more colleges and their athletic

programs, you will start to define your criteria of what you want in a school.

- College coaches are likely to assume that the student athlete is not interested in their program if initial communication is ignored. You never want to give anyone a bad first impression or make them think that you are not interested in their program.

It's common courtesy and takes a small amount of time to respond to a coach who has contacted you. Who knows? One of these colleges may turn out to be the one you decide to attend!

Peter Kim
Head Coach Women's Soccer
Assistant Coach Men's and Women's Track and Field
Middlebury College

Don't wait to be picked out of a crowd. Many athletes make the mistake of letting fate decide which coaches recruit them, rather than taking matters into their own hands. Find the schools that are interesting possibilities for you, then reach out directly to those coaches. Be politely persistent with contacts, but remember to brush up on the recruiting rules that dictate when and how coaches can connect with you. Club coaches and DOCs can be great resources, but be careful about those who will try to steer you toward a particular kind of school for the purpose of enhancing the club's status. This process is about helping you find the right college fit … for YOU.

Tips for Freshman Year:

- Make a list of colleges you would like to attend (10-20) and send them to your coach.

- Create your player profile and send to your team manager and coach.

- Get involved in school activities (student government, NHS, clubs, community service, etc.).

- Focus on grades.

- Communicate with coaches about upcoming showcases for the year.

- Start building a highlight video.

- Meet with your coach about your list of schools to classify the major schools of interest.

- Attend College Nights offered by your club or school.

- Attend four to five showcases a year (make sure to write to at least 10 coaches for each showcase).

- Visit colleges as much as possible throughout the year (no communication with coaches).
- Attend College ID camps at schools of interest.

HIGH SCHOOL SOPHOMORE YEAR

Keep Your Grades Up

Think of yourself as a student first, and an athlete second. Keeping your grades up will make you more desirable as a recruit. As a future collegiate student-athlete, you will be juggling academics with your sport. A strong academic performance in high school demonstrates your ability to be successful as a collegiate student-athlete.

Refine your list of colleges

Keep researching and adding information to your database of colleges on their academic and athletic programs.

1. **Visit a range of schools** near you even if they aren't at the top of your list. Looking at a variety of schools gives

you an opportunity to compare, and then you can use this information to widen your search geographically. Attend an info session, event, or go on a campus tour. If you can't get to the campus in person, try a virtual tour. There might be college fairs at your high school. Attend those as well even though the coach won't be there. You can let the Admissions staff at the fair pass on your interest to the coach at their college.

2. **Keep notes** including photos of each school visit. Colleges will start to blur together quickly. Use your checklist of top priorities in a college. The notes should include your reaction to the school. What did you notice? What did you like and dislike? What things surprised you? What programs mentioned caught your attention? Once the time comes to submit your applications, you will have a helpful list to reflect back on and evaluate your fit at each school. This is particularly helpful for college applications with supplemental essays.

3. **Get advice** from peers, siblings, family members, older students, older siblings of friends, high school and club coaches, and alumni too, if available.

4. **Keep visiting schools!** Each college visit will give you more information about what a school is like. You will also start to get a sense of what matters to you. As you figure out the factors that are important to you, you can expand

your school list by finding colleges that fit your criteria.

5. **Find the right fit for *you*.** You may find that it takes time to figure out what type of college feels comfortable to you, and balances your academic, athletic, and social requirements.

Sophie Bengochea
Women's Beach Volleyball
University of South Carolina

I started playing volleyball in third grade through my Catholic school on a YMCA team, and then I switched to club volleyball. I played club for one year. The summer after 5th grade, I was introduced to beach volleyball. I loved it so much that in 6th grade, I switched to beach volleyball. I actually was the first person to completely transition from indoor to beach volleyball in San Antonio.

My club team would host tournaments that college coaches attended so it was probably in 8th grade that college coaches first saw me play. I didn't initiate contact until later on because it was just too early. My recruiting process began in freshman year when I contacted five or six coaches.

Texas Christian University was the first college that I visited. It's near me and I grew up going to their camps.

They were the first to give me an offer. Once word got out that I had an offer, coaches began to speed things up by trying to get me to visit. During the fall of my sophomore year, I visited six schools. During the visits I talked to the coaches one-on-one about what it would be like to play on their team as well as future scholarships.

The South Carolina coach didn't actually see me until later in the process. My first call with the coaches there lasted for an hour, and we just got along really well. I think my parents knew for a long time that I would end up there, but they let me figure it out for myself. Once I visited their campus the fall of my sophomore year, I knew that it was a place that felt comfortable to me, and that I would be okay moving and living there.

Take the PSAT

The PSAT test will give a prospective coach an idea of how you might score on the SAT or ACT test. The PSAT test also awards National Merit scholarships to the top 1% of students, about 15,000 students. If you are interested in getting the recognition of a National Merit Scholar and potential scholarship money, it's worth scheduling time to study for the PSAT test.

Unlike the SAT, which requires online registration through the College Board, **you will register for the PSAT through your own high school which will have its own sign-up process.** Your high school will inform their students when the PSAT registration deadline is, and then give instructions on how to register and pay for the test.

Registering for the PSAT test will generally require basic information including your full name, home address, phone number, email address, grade level, and student ID number (if applicable).

The cost of the PSAT is $16 per student, but some schools might cover all or part of the fee. Schools might also charge more than $16 per student in order to cover the cost of proctors and test administrators. Talk to your high school counselor if you wish to receive financial assistance for the fee. Some high schools offer financial assistance for those who qualify.

Your school will select the date on which it will administer the PSAT. Most schools choose the primary date, but some might instead administer the PSAT on one of the two alternate dates should the primary date not work well with the school's schedule.

If your high school isn't going to offer the PSAT, you may take the test at another nearby school.

SAT or ACT

If you are not sure which standardized test to take, you might want to take diagnostic tests for both the SAT and ACT to decide. Many colleges super score the SAT test which means they will accept the highest score for each section of the SAT, out of all the official tests that you take.

The ACT includes a science section, which the SAT does not have. Starting in September 2020, the ACT introduced new options. For students who have taken the ACT test more than once, they now have the option to retake individual section tests (English, math, reading, science, and/or writing) rather than taking the entire test again. ACT will also permit students to "super score" by combining their best scores on subject tests.

There are other differences between the two tests, but the best way to decide is to take both diagnostic tests and analyze your results.

Keep a Record of Athletic Achievements

Continue to keep track of your individual and team athletic achievements. You will be using this information to create your athletic resume.

Plan College ID Clinics

Use your college wish list to decide which college ID clinics to attend, if possible. This is a good way to see what the college program and coach are like, and to see where you stand in terms of interest from the coach.

Jude Braithwaite
Men's Club Soccer
American University

I started playing soccer at six-years-old when my family lived abroad in China and then Singapore. When I came to the United States, I played club soccer in middle school and high school. It was through U.S. club soccer that I began the college soccer recruiting process by attending college ID camps. That style of evaluation really wasn't for me. It wasn't necessarily the pressure, but I really hated the feeling of always being judged. It turned me off from pursuing playing soccer in college. Instead, I focused more on my high school soccer team because it was where I had the most fun. I ended up quitting club soccer by senior year of high school because I decided to focus on going to college based on my academic interests, International Diplomacy, rather than my athletic ability.

I didn't want to give up soccer completely so I thought club soccer at college would be a good way to continue playing without the stress and pressure of varsity soccer. At my college, sixty players tried out for five spots and I ended up making the team. It was not at all what I expected. There was no pressure to go to practice or games. It's more for the fun of it rather than the competition though it still feels competitive. The club soccer program at American University is a six-week season with optional practices twice a week, and two games against three teams on a Saturday or a Sunday. There is a coach and assistant coach. I thought the coaches were terrific and they were very flexible in terms of scheduling (and rescheduling) games to accommodate our schedules. We competed against colleges in the DC area, and travel as far as Baltimore. I really enjoyed club soccer. It was a great way to meet people including upperclassmen. I plan to play club soccer this spring. Current team members automatically retain their spot.

In part, I do wish that I had tried harder at ID camps to get recruited. I do feel like I could have gone further than I did. At that time, I was prepared to give up soccer for academics and I was willing to go to a college that didn't have soccer. I would advise kids that the recruiting process sucks but ID camps are the best way to get recruited. For someone who played soccer as much I did, playing three times a week with games on the weekend, it has been hard not to play soccer year round. Though to be fair, not all colleges have the International Diplomacy program that I am interested in with varsity soccer programs that would have been a good fit for me. Everything is a trade-off.

Watch Local College Games

If any of the colleges on your list are local, you will want to watch them play. Not only will you see their level and style of play and coaching, but you can notice specifics that you can reference in a cover letter or during your college visit to the coaching staff. For example, it could be an exciting come-from-behind victory, their style of play, how the team interacted with their young fans, or charity work that the team is involved with.

Kia McNeill
Head Coach Women's Soccer
Brown University
Ivy League Champions 2019
Coach of the Year 2019

DO attend the games of any schools that you are considering (or watch online). A lot of prospective student-athletes say, "I think I would be a great fit for your program," but have never seen the program play. If you are a technical center-midfielder that shows best when the ball is at your feet, and a school you are interested in plays very direct and bypasses the midfield, maybe this wouldn't be the best program for you. From a recruiting perspective it is good for prospective student-athletes to be knowledgeable about the program they are looking at – know the conference, the record, key players, etc. (Especially the more involved/deeper you get in the recruiting process).

Social Media

Review all your social media posts and comments, even those set to private, to make sure that there is nothing negative from middle school and high school. Keep your online presence professional and assume that coaches are evaluating you based on your social media presence.

Register with the NCAA Eligibility Center

Students who plan to compete in athletics at the Division I or Division II college level must register with the NCAA Eligibility Center. Division III does not use the Eligibility Center. There is a $90 registration fee for students from the

U.S., its territories, and Canada. The fee for students from other countries is $150. Some students may be eligible for a fee waiver.

You will need the following to register:

- Email address that you check often and will be active after you complete high school.

- Education history with names and dates of high schools attended.

- Sports participation history including teams and events and information about any individuals who have advised you or marketed your skills.

To pay online you will need to use a credit card. The steps for registering on line are as follows:

1. Visit **https://web3.ncaa.org/ecwr3/** and read the two account descriptions.

2. If you plan to compete at an NCAA Division I or II school, select the "Create an Account" button and follow the prompts. NCA DIII schools do not require you to go through the eligibility center process.

3. On the next page, provide a valid email address to create either account and begin the registration process. Be sure you provide an email address that you check frequently and will be active even after you complete high school.

4. Check your email inbox for an email containing a verification code and return to **https://web3.ncaa.org/ecwr3/**. Enter your verification code and continue registering.

5. Complete the Account, Basic Information and Contact pages.

6. Certification Accounts will be prompted to pay the nonrefundable registration fee. Students have 30 days after receiving a verification code to pay before their account is dropped out of the system. After submitting payment, return to your Dashboard to complete registration. If you are applying for a fee waiver, your authorized high school official will submit it after completing registration.

7. Enter your most recent high school information. Please include all schools, even if you did not receive grades or credits. If you have completed coursework at home, you may or may not be a **home school student** for the purposes of NCAA initial-eligibility.

8. After entering school information, Certification Accounts will be taken to the Sports page. Please select the sport(s) you plan to compete in and continue to answer the Sports questions.

9. After completing the School section (Profile Pages) and Sports section (Certification Accounts) you will be taken back to your Dashboard.

Sample Email to Coaches

What should your cover letter say? The communication should be short as all your details will be in your player profile.

Here are some guidelines:

First paragraph: State the purpose of your letter by introducing yourself and what specifically you want. Include your full name, high school, club team you play on, and current grade level.

Second paragraph: Personalize the letter to the coach by referencing recent games that you watched and what impressed you about the team. Explain why you are choosing this school and/or team using specific examples. Include details of your interaction with the school including quantifying the number of visits, overnights, camps you participated in, and games that you watched.

Third paragraph: This is where you make the case for why you are qualified to be on the team. Give details on your athletic and academic achievements and include your high school athletic experience, years of varsity experience, club and high school team accomplishments, and personal awards. If you know what academic field you are interested in, include that after making sure that the college offers it.

Last paragraph: State the actions that you will take next. For example, if you plan to follow-up with a phone call, state the timeframe within which you plan to call. Let the coach know of any showcase tournaments you will be attending with your club or high school team. This is a great way to be seen by a prospective coach. Remember to let the coach know your jersey number, where applicable, so he or she can easily identify you.

Make your email short and to the point. You simply want to introduce yourself to the coach as a prospective student-athlete. Make sure you proofread carefully so that there are no typos. Double check that the school and coach's name is spelled correctly. Include information to get in touch with you, such as your email address, phone number, and home address.

Be sure to track every interaction including letters sent, dates, and responses. Mark on your calendar the action steps you committed to and be sure to follow through.

John Kennaday
Head Coach Men's Varsity Golf
San Jose State

Don't cut and paste letters to every coach or every school that you want to go to. Half the time, my name is misspelled or the school is incorrect in the letter or email. **Half the time!** It's great to write a personal note or handwritten letter, but make sure that you get things right.

General Introduction Sample Email 1

Dear Coach,

My name is Alex Thompson and I am currently a sophomore at Newton High School in Newton, Massachusetts.

Congratulations on winning the Ivy League! I enjoyed watching Brown versus Harvard and thought your team did a brilliant job of pressuring their backline to create scoring opportunities. I fell in love with Brown University when I participated in the *Introduction to Premed* program last summer, and I plan to attend your ID clinic this winter.

I am the starting outside midfield on my high school soccer team, playing the number seven, and was awarded all-league. My team won the state championship last year and was the runner up in 2018. We are currently ranked second in the country. I also play for SAZ United where I captain the team.

I am interested in majoring in Biology with a minor in Journalism and feel that Brown's open curriculum and strong liberal arts program make this a good fit. I would appreciate receiving information from you.

Thank you for your time.

Sincerely,

Alex Thompson
123 Anywhere Lane
Newton, MA 02468

AThompson16@gmail.com
617-877-8777

{The names are fictitious and are not based on real people.}

General Introduction Sample Email 2

Dear Coach,

My name is Alex Thompson and I am currently a sophomore at Newton High School in Newton, Massachusetts.

I am very interested in your college as it is a good fit for me both academically and athletically. Could you please send me information about your school and the soccer program?

I am the starting outside midfield on my high school soccer team, playing the number seven, and was awarded all-league. My team won the state championship last year and were the runner up in 2018. We are currently ranked second in the country. I also play for SAZ United where I captain the team. I have played on the first team since U-14. My team won the NPL Regionals and went on to Colorado to win the National championships. My coach, Wally Tyler, said he would be glad to speak with you on my behalf.

Academically, I am a strong student. I have a 1440 SAT and have an unweighted 3.9 GPA with a rigorous course load. In addition to athletics, I performed in our school's musical, am a member of my church choir group, and volunteer at the food bank in my community.

Thank you for your time. I look forward to hearing back from you.

Sincerely,

Alex Thompson
123 Anywhere Lane
Newton, MA 02468

AThompson16@gmail.com
617-877-8777

General Introduction Sample Email 3

Dear Coaches Denton, Gill, See and Stanton,

Hello, my name is Alex Thompson and I am in the graduating class of 2021 at Newton High School in Newton, Massachusetts. Firstly, congratulations on a great season!

Setting multiple school records and having one of your players recognized for their efforts and placed on the Atlantic-10 second team is quite an accomplishment. I am very interested in one day playing soccer at Davidson College and your extensive Health Sciences Program really pulled me in to want to know more about your school.

I play defense on the SAZ 2002 United team, coached by Chris Sharma but I am guest playing for his 2001 DA team at the CASL tournament November 22nd - 24th and I really hope you will be able to watch me play. I am number seven and will be wearing a red or white jersey. I will also be playing in the GPS tournament the following weekend here in Massachusetts.

This year I was made Captain of my high school team and I am proud to say we are currently ranked #10 in New England. Yesterday, we played our last game, finishing up our season with an impressive record of 14-4. We fought some hard battles from beginning to end but our team has been dominating, and I am thrilled to say we made play-offs and will be hosting quarterfinals!

I have attached a copy of my resume below with more information about my current academics and extracurriculars. I will also keep you updated with my grades as well as any soccer updates. I hope to hear from you soon and I am eager to learn more about your program and goals. Go Wildcats!

CASL Tournament Link:
https://soccer.sincsports.com/team/team.

Game Times:
11/22/19 – 1:30 PM
11/23/19 – 3:20 PM
11/24/19 – 11:40 AM

GPS Schedule Link:

**https://www.globalpremiersoccer.net/
gpsfathersdayinvitationalandcollegeshowcase**

Thank you,

Alex Thompson #8
Class of 2021
617-123-4567
AlexThompson16@gmail.com

123 Anywhere Lane
Newton, MA 02468

Athletic Resume

Your athletic resume includes your basic personal information and athletic accomplishments. It also provides a history of your activity in the sport with information about your past teams, camps, tournaments and other experiences. Include athletic accomplishments in other sports as well.

Include your scholastic accomplishments, standardized test scores if available, and extracurricular activities. Coaches are looking at you both for your athletic achievements and versatility and as a whole person in terms of what you can bring to the school and athletic program.

Include:

- Name
- Graduation Date
- Address
- Home and Cell Phone Numbers
- Email address
- Height
- Weight
- Date of Birth
- High School Information (name of high school, address of high school, high school phone number, high school coach, coach's phone number, guidance counselor name, school fax number)
- Academic Achievements
- Club name, position, and jersey number (if applicable)
- Athletic Achievements (club team, high school team, other sports)
- Extracurricular Activities

Sample Resume

Name/Graduation Date/Photo

Address

Cell/Email Address

ACADEMIC ACHIEVEMENTS

- SAT 1300/ACT 30

- National Honor Society: 11, 12

- 3.99 Cumulative GPA at School Name

- Spanish Honor Society: 11, 12

- Sophomore year: 5 honors classes

- Junior year: AP Language Comp, AP US History, Honors Pre-Calculus, Honors Anatomy, Honors Spanish IV, Honors Just Choices

- Senior year: AP Literature, AP Spanish, AP Government, Honors Calculus, Honors Physics, Honors World Religions

ATHLETIC ACHIEVEMENTS

- Starting Defender/Midfielder Varsity Soccer: 9, 10, 11, 12

- Elected Co-Captain Varsity Soccer: 11, 12

- Varsity Soccer Award of Excellence for Exemplary Display of Sportsmanship, Ethics and Integrity: 11

- Club Team Name Soccer: 9, 10, 11, 12
- Played on the same team for the same club since age seven
  - Selected for Region I ID Camp and Ryder Cup Tournament
  - ODP National Camp and Region I Pool Player
  - Massachusetts ODP Player
  - Team Accomplishments:
    - US Youth Soccer National qualifiers two years in a row
    - National League Champions
    - Region 1 Premier League Champions
    - Massachusetts State Cup Champions
    - NPL/NEP Champions

EXTRA-CURRICULAR ACTIVITIES AND SERVICE

- Peer Mentor: 11, 12
  - Played a major role in setting a welcoming tone for the school
  - Selected to serve in freshman homerooms to help make a smooth transition to NDA by answering questions, giving advice, and introducing them to new friends

- Helped to plan programs including orientation, freshman day, and events with boys' schools
- Key Club: 9, 10, 11, 12
  - In-school service group that serves as official representatives to the public at Open Houses and other school events by interacting with prospective students and parents
- Seva Volunteer Trip to Haiti with Devoted to Children: 11
  - Spent time with, and helped provide for, the children in the family home; these children were either abandoned or had families who couldn't afford to look after them due to extreme poverty
  - Worked with the community on local projects
  - Helped at a local school with their after-school program

REFERENCES

- Coach Name/Title cell number email address
- Coaching Director Cell number email address

John Kennaday
Head Coach Men's Varsity Golf
San Jose State

Don't overestimate your ability. If a player realizes that he has a lot to learn when he or she comes in, it's a good place to start. I recommend an attitude of humble confidence. If you think you are going to come in and dominate, you are going to get into big trouble.

Do I Need a Video?

College coaches are looking for different ways to evaluate prospective student-athletes and watching an initial highlight video is one of them. This video will merely serve as an introduction and an opportunity for the coaches to get an indication of who you are and what type of player you are.

Normally it will not be the only way you will get recruited but a good video can peak interest. You want to dedicate time to make a high-quality video.

The gamer video should be taped from a high angle, ideally using a tripod or top of a press box.

Getting footage from multiple games is a good idea and will allow you more film to choose highlights from. In terms of gathering your film, most high schools and clubs are videotaping games and using it as a learning tool for video analysis. Speak to your coach to see if it is available. If not, you may need to hire an outside company. In terms of when to send a college coach your video, I would wait until the end of your sophomore year or the beginning of your junior year and then update it accordingly. It is also never too late!

If you just decided to play college sports in your senior year, there is still time to get clipping and editing.

There are three main types of recruiting videos. Depending on what sport you play, one may work better than the other to showcase your talent. **All videos should have an opening clip with a still action shot, your full name, graduation date, jersey number, club name, your position, and email/phone number.**

The three forms of video recruiting are:

Highlight Tape

The highlight tape should be three to five minutes in duration. This type of film is the most popular in the recruiting process. The clips should show a little before your highlight and a little bit after. This way the coach can see how the play developed and how it was completed. For example, throwing a Hail Mary pass at the wrong time or nowhere close to the receiver may not be a highlight, but one that was done at a crucial moment, successfully caught, and led to the winning touchdown would be a highlight. It is also important not to show the same type of skill set over and over again. The goal is to show the complete player.

A highlight video should show clips that showcase you according to your skills and position specific expectations/ responsibilities. A coach will review any video of you based on position specific expectations.

You should ensure your highlight video is current. As time passes, substitute old clips with recent ones to keep your video fresh.

Remember to keep this tape no more than five minutes long and highlight your best clips at the beginning. Captivate the coaches' attention early so they are more compelled to watch your whole tape.

Skills Tape

A skills tape is similar to a highlight tape. It should also be three to five minutes in duration. Pitches in baseball or goal-keepers in various sports often take advantage of a skills tape.

A skills tape is one that shows a specific skill set being repeated and often not in a game format but in a training session where someone is taping the coach working with the player. For example, a goal-keeper may show his or her ability on crosses, and then their quickness and footwork with a cone drill. They may also show their vertical jump, distribution from punts, goal-kicks, and balls played back to them.

In a skills tape, you want to show your competency using both sides. For example, in lacrosse, include footage diving to the left and the right, and throwing a lacrosse ball from the left and the right side of your body. In basketball, show a lay-up leading with your left hand and your right hand.

Often a skills tape is combined into a hybrid tape showing some game highlights as well.

Remember to still keep it under the magic five minutes.

Game Footage Tape

You may have had the best 10 minutes in a game that you have ever played. So, you may just send the 10 minutes of game footage to coaches. This may be just enough to peak their interest and ask for the whole game tape or at least communicate their interest to you.

Game footage is also a good alternative if you don't feel comfortable editing tape.

Regardless of what method of video you use to be recruited, make sure the resolution is of high level. If your video includes background music, make sure that it is "clean" and upbeat.

Circling, highlighting, freeze-framing on you is helpful for the coaches to hone in on you immediately.

Uploading the footage in HUDL or YouTube are the most popular ways to share your video link. Make sure you send it to the head coach, assistant coach, recruiting coordinator, and if there is a position specific coach, to them as well. You have worked hard to create your video, let's make sure you get seen!

The Role of Parents in Recruiting Process

Parents are being evaluated as much as athletes, and this is the case of "less is more." The coach is recruiting the athlete for the program, not the parents or guardians. It's really important to let the athlete develop the relationship with the coach. As a parent, when in doubt, err on the side of invisibility.

Top 10 Things Parents Should Not Do

1. *Don't initiate contact with a coach.* It's your child's job to show interest in a program. The email should come from the athlete.

2. *Don't call the coach.* The coach does not want to hear from you.

3. *Don't brag* about your child's athletic skills.

4. *Don't talk too much.* The relationship is between the athlete and the coaching staff.

5. *Don't be overbearing.* It's not your job to ask if your child will start or how much playing time to expect. This raises a red flag that there is a seed of dissatisfaction already being sown.

6. *Don't be rowdy in the stands.* If you are making an impression in the stands, it is probably the wrong kind.

7. *Don't belittle your spouse or talk down to your child.* A negative style of communication will be noted.

8. *Wait outside if asked.* If the coach asks the parents to wait outside during the meeting, happily agree.

9. *Don't talk about how you coached your child.* Now is not the time for affirmation about your role in developing your child's athletic ability.

10. *Don't talk about your athlete's faults.* It's not your job to help the coach evaluate their prospects.

Top 10 Things Parents Should Do

1. *Proofread* your child's communication.

2. *Cheer for their team.* Be positive and don't coach from the sidelines.

3. *Be respectful.* You never know who is watching and who has the coach's ear. Be respectful and considerate of all staff that you encounter from maintenance to trainers to

referees.

4. *Thank the coaching staff* for their time.

5. *Support your child.* Perhaps your child just needs you to be their driver. Maybe your child needs encouragement to initiate and stay in contact with the coaches.

6. *Help your child come up with five questions* to ask the coaching staff concerning information that is not on the website. Encourage them to write it down for reference during their meeting.

7. *Encourage independence.* Let your child converse with the coaching staff and express his or her own opinions. Help your athlete set-up and maintain their tracking and calendar system.

8. *Help your child practice leaving phone messages* for the coach.

9. *Be encouraging.* There will be communication glitches or miscommunication during this process that might cause your athlete to ride an emotional roller coaster. Help them understand that there are many options in this long process.

10. *Be flexible.* The road to recruitment can be long and bumpy. There is no singular "perfect college or team". The right college or sport will eventually surface.

Kia McNeill
Head Coach Women's Soccer
Brown University
Ivy League Champions 2019
Coach of the Year 2019

DON'T take over your daughter's or son's recruiting process. Let them be an active part of trying to navigate what types of schools and soccer programs interest them. Remember, this is a school where *they* are going to be for four years, not you. Therefore, the priorities they want in a school should be about them. Where parents can be helpful is by trying to help their child navigate what things to consider: distance from home, school size, urban vs. rural campus settings, concentration offerings, playing style of the program. Open the discussion to talking through these things, but don't make the decisions for them.

Early Reads

An early read gives the coach as well as yourself an opportunity to get a preliminary "read" from the institution's Admissions Office to see if you are an admissible PSA based on the most recent transcript and test scores provided. This means, provided that you continue to do the work in the classroom and maintain the standards that you've achieved so far, that you are an admissible student.

Each school has a different policy with their Admissions Office. The amount of leeway each school has will vary. Typically, the more academic the school is, the less wiggle room they will have with athletes.

Tips for Sophomore Year:

- Update your list of colleges of interest (list should contain at least 10-15 schools).

- Sign up and take the PSAT (add scores to your player profile).

- Update your player profile with any new information (awards, GPA, PSAT scores etc.).

- Focus on grades.

- Complete college questionnaires for prospective recruits.

- Stay in communication with coaches about upcoming showcases for the year.

- If applying to DI and DII schools, direct college coach communication can take place from June 15th (excluding football, women's basketball, baseball, lacrosse, and softball. For these sports, direct college coach communication cannot take place until Sept 1st of junior year).

- Attend College Night offered by your club or high school.

- Starting on June 15th prior to your junior year, direct college coach communication can take place.

- Attend four to five showcases a year (make sure to write to at least 10 coaches for each showcase).

- If you are applying to DII and DII schools, go on unofficial visits to colleges as much as possible throughout the year.

- Attend College ID camps at schools of interest.

Jacob Jampel
Men's Nordic Ski
Williams College

My recruiting journey was unconventional. I started Nordic Skiing in fifth grade but I didn't realize that I wanted to compete in college until my sophomore year in high school when my sister competed on a really fun team in college.

The college ski circuit on the east coast, EISA, doesn't allow for full ride scholarships so schools tend to recruit more locally. I really wanted to ski in the EISA league because I felt that I had a shot to make a team.

I emailed all the coaches on the East Coast very informally

and set up meetings with them. I visited the NESCACs as well as Harvard and Dartmouth which have Nordic Ski teams. I ended up liking the NESCACs more.

A lot of the colleges said that I could try out but because I wasn't a top, top skier in my high school league, I wasn't getting the top recruiting spots. Some coaches suggested that I could use another year.

I decided to join the Sun Valley Ski Education Program which had a specific program for high schoolers to train for one year before college. I trained six days a week and also worked part time at the YMCA and at a burger restaurant. The extra year really helped me with growth and maturity. This really helped me balance academics with training when I got to college.

My advice to high school Nordic Skiers is that there are lots of choices even though it can feel like it's really constricted in terms of the number of colleges on the Eastern Circuit. There is always a place that you can find where you will be happy. It's important to realize that if it doesn't work out at one school, the likelihood that it will at another is high.

HIGH SCHOOL JUNIOR YEAR

Keep your grades up!

Be prepared to communicate with college coaches over the phone and continue to put academics first and perform well in school.

Narrow Down Your College Wish List

Narrow down your list to 10 or so colleges and communicate regularly with these coaches.

Take the SAT or the ACT

Take a diagnostic to decide which test is right for you. Schedule to take the SAT or the ACT. Leave enough time in case you want to take the test more than once. You may want to study on your own or take a test prep class prior to sitting the test. Kahn Academy offers free online test prep:

www.khanacademy.org/sat. There is also free practice on **www.crackact.com** and **www.cracksat.com**.

Check Your Status with the NCAA or NAIA Clearinghouse

Confirm that you are registered with the NCAA or NAIA Clearinghouse and are on track to meet eligibility requirements.

Contact Coaches

On June 15th after your sophomore year for most sports, Division I & II coaches can now contact you.

Send coaches on your list updates on your tournaments/meets/games so that they can observe you. Also send them your updated athletic resume.

Schedule calls with coaches in advance. This way you will guarantee that both of you are available to connect.

Keep a list of Top Five questions to ask and make sure the information is not on the website.

You will also want to understand how often each coach wants to be contacted. Ask each coach individually and note it in your tracking system. Also use your calendar to note when you need to follow up with coaches.

Lucy Jenks
Track and Field
Stanford University

The timeline for recruiting for track and field is very different than for soccer. I started talking to coaches during the winter of my junior year. I reached out to coaches and emailed some schools that I was interested in.

Most coaches communicated to me through Instagram. They would follow me and DM me. A lot of running coaches use Instagram for recruiting which is different from soccer. As the year went on, more coaches started reaching out to me.

Play in College Showcase Tournaments, Summer Tournaments and ID Clinics

Be sure to let the coaches on your list know about college showcase and summer tournaments/meets/games that you are attending. Consider attending ID clinics at a few of the colleges on your short list.

You will want to follow-up with the coaching staff after attending their ID clinic. This is an opportunity to express interest in their program and get feedback on where you stand while you are still fresh in their mind. Send an email within a few days after the event.

How to Write a Follow-Up Email

1. Send an email if possible

2. Use a clear subject line

3. Thank them for coming to your athletic event

4. Ask for feedback

5. Ask for upcoming ID clinic information

6. Keep it brief

7. Focus on why you are a good fit

8. Ask questions

9. Mention a visit

Sample Email to Coaches after Attending Their ID Clinic

Dear Coach Jones and Coach Hawkins,

Congrats on your NCAA bid, I'll be watching the selection show today to see who you draw in the first round. I work with Alison Foley and she has been encouraging me to look at Brown and all the good things you are doing with the program. I hope to contribute in the future.

I had so much fun at your clinic yesterday and loved your entire coaching staff and everything about your program. I was wondering if you have any feedback about my play from what you saw this weekend and where you are at with your 2021 recruiting class.

I am also attaching the rest of my schedule for this season below and hope to see you at one of the games if it is possible.

Go Bears!

Game #	Home	Score	Visitor	Score	Date and Time	Location
6541736	NEFC U-18/19	0	Penn Fusion Soccer Academy U-18/19	0	11/16/2019 12:30pm	NEFC Park 2
6541767	NEFC U-18/19	0	PA Classics U-18/19	0	11/17/2019	NEFC Park 1

Best,

Alex Thompson '21
123 Anywhere Lane
Newton, MA 02468

AThompson16@gmail.com
617-877-8777

Visit Colleges

Make unofficial visits (at your expense) to selected schools. Schedule a meeting with the coach and watch the team play if possible. You might be invited for an official visit. If so, starting on August 1 prior to junior year for Division I & II of most sports, players can make up to five official visits.

Kevin Bletzer
Varsity Football
Boston College

I was a college football player at Boston College from 2014-2018. My recruiting process was not much different from anyone else's: stressful. My parents and I were in a foreign territory that none of us had traveled before. None of us had any idea of what to do.

My recruiting actually started when I was a freshman or sophomore in high school but not for football, for lacrosse. Lacrosse recruitment starts much earlier than football. My summer lacrosse team went to a lot of showcases that universities from all over the country were attending. So, for lacrosse, I got exposure early, unlike football. I visited a couple of schools interested in offering me lacrosse scholarships, but I realized that I wanted to play football in college. People thought I was crazy because I had a lot of offers from some of the best universities and teams in the country, but I knew what I wanted and stuck with it.

While I got to experience the recruiting process through lacrosse, I actually had a different experience for football recruitment. Football recruitment got a little tricky because I wasn't getting the same exposure to college coaches that I had in lacrosse.

Luckily, my high school football team attended the BC football camp every year since I was in 8th grade. Without the BC camp, I never would have gone to college for football.

Going into my senior year, I had a great camp and workout. The day after camp, BC called and offered me a scholarship. I was honestly lucky because BC was a school I wanted to go to since I was five. I grew up in the area and had season tickets for as long as I can remember.

Recruiting can be a very stressful time like it was for myself. If I were to do it all over again, I would go to more football camps. It's a great way to visit colleges and experience what it is like there. Coaches are also able to see your talent. It's the best way to kill two birds with one stone!

My second piece of advice would be to relax. While this

is a big decision it doesn't have to be rushed or stressed. Everything will work out. You do not have to decide the rest of your life right this second!

Third and most importantly, my advice would be to do what YOU want to do. All too often I see these parents literally making decisions for their kids and I could see the life drain from the kid. While parents do want what's best for you, it is YOU that has to make that decision. That's probably the only thing I did well in my recruiting process. I knew from when I was a little kid I wanted to play football. The stress in recruiting came between my parents and me because of this. My father thought I should play lacrosse because I had offers already. My mother just all together did not think that I would get into college because my SAT score wasn't very high. But I knew what I wanted and stuck with it. It was tough trying to get them on board because, like I said, parents want what's best for you, and they thought they were doing the right thing. At the end of the day, it has to be my decision because it is my life and I'm the only one living it!

So just do those things in recruiting and it'll be a breeze! Best of luck to whoever reads this in their recruiting process. I hope that I helped one person even just a tiny bit!

Plan Unofficial College Visits

Some of these items pertain to NCAA schools only. It's always best to check with the umbrella organization to verify recruitment rules. The governing organizations meet on a regular basis and can change rules.

The best way to learn about a college or university is to visit it. While on campus you can get a feel for the school. Try to visit while school is in session. If you visit over the summer, keep in mind many colleges do offer summer programs, therefore the students you see on campus may not be full-time students. At many Division III schools, no summer classes are offered.

Sample Questions that Generally Work for Any School:

- Tell me about undergraduate housing options.

- What do you think of the food?

- How diverse is the student population?

- What percentage of students are from out of state?

- Will you be visiting my high school in the coming year?

- Do you allow a gap year?

- How diverse is the faculty?

- What percentage of students travel abroad?

- What percentage of students are from [my state]?

- How would you describe the personality of your college?

- What are some of the things that make your college unique?

- What are the most popular student clubs and organizations?

While on campus, why not schedule a little time to visit with the coach? Meeting with a coach is a great opportunity to ask questions about the school and their sports program. It may also help you decide if you like the coach. This is a great time to market yourself to the coach. It is also important for college coaches to be honest with you.

You also should consider bringing a parent. Your parents are more likely to ask questions that you won't. Use this visit to talk with the coaching staff to mutually get to know each other.

Official Visit

An official visit is when the college pays for all or part of the athlete's expenses for the visit, including travel expenses. This is often an overnight visit where the athlete gets to meet the coaching staff and team. A member of the team is frequently the host for each athlete. There may be other recruits visiting as well. The itinerary includes sitting in on a class, and possibly an athletic event. It is also possible to meet with professors.

The objective is to provide you with a better feel for the school and life on campus.

Athletes are limited to five official visits. The prerequisites for an official visit are the completion of the SAT or ACT, and high school transcripts. In sports other than baseball, basketball, football, lacrosse, and softball, a prospective student-athlete may not take an expense-paid visit earlier than August 1st of his or her junior year in high school.

An official visit is a recruiting event meant to get the athlete excited about the school and the athletic program. It's an opportunity for the athlete and parents to get to know the coaching staff, team members, as well as life on the campus. Ultimately the intent is to figure out if this is a good fit. Use this time to get to know everyone by talking to as many people as possible. Take notes during meetings and also journal your thoughts at the end of each day. Remember, there is no such thing as a bad question!

Planning for Your Official Visit

- Research if you know anyone on campus, even if he or she is not an athlete
- Ask what to bring
- Decide if a parent is coming with you
- Ask to meet with Financial Aid

- Ask to meet with a professor in your area of interest

- Ask to meet with Admissions to understand procedure

- Prepare questions to ask coaching staff, team members, professors, Admissions, and financial aid

- Take notes during these meetings

- Write up your impressions at the end of each day

- Players and students can give you accurate information about what it is like to attend school here

- Write a personalized thank you note to everyone that you met with

Questions to Ask College Coaches

Many of these questions are from the NCAA resources.[13]

Questions to Ask About Athletics

- How do you see me contributing to the team?

- Is there a specific position (or event) that you have in mind for me?

- How many other athletes are you considering for this position? Who are they?

....

[13] 2008 NCAA College-Bound Student-Athlete publication, pages 23-28

- Will I be redshirted my freshman year?

- What are practices and conditioning sessions like during pre-season and off-season?

- How would you describe your coaching style and philosophy?

- How would you describe the team culture?

- What are the team rules set by coaching staff?

- What happens when team rules are broken?

- What does the practice and team travel schedule look like?

- What is the difference between in-season, out-of-season, and summer training?

- What is the support for student-athletes including academic and social-emotional?

- If there is a mandatory class or lab that conflicts with practice, how do you handle that?

- Does the team have priority housing and course selection?

- Have you ever increased scholarships due to a player's positive influence on or off the field?

- Does the college provide medical insurance or must I purchase it?

- What is the cost of the medical insurance?

- What does your sports medicine department provide?

- If I am injured while competing, who is responsible for my medical expenses?

- Do you feel that your program is supported at an equivalent level to your competitors in the conference?

- How long do you plan to remain as the coach?

Questions About College Life

- What is a typical day for a student-athlete?

- What percentage of students are part of Greek life?

- Are you allowed to join a fraternity or sorority?

- What percentage of students live on campus?

- What are the dorms or housing options?

- What are the residence halls like?

- How many students are there in a room?

- Do I have to room with a player on the team or is my roommate a non-athlete?

- Can I pick my roommate?

- Do student-athletes have to live on campus? Are there any exceptions?

- What is the social scene like on campus?

- Is there diversity on campus?

- Is there a lot of interaction between people of different races and socio-economic status?

- Are there cliques on campus?

- What do students do off-campus for entertainment?

- How easy is it to get off-campus?

- How many hours do students study per week?

Questions to Ask About Academics

- What are the most popular majors?

- Is it possible to meet with a professor in my area of interest?

- How accessible are professors? Will they meet with you outside of office hours?

- Are there opportunities to work on research projects with professors?

- Is there a mentorship program?

- What percentage of players that are on scholarship graduate?

- Are there study hall requirements for freshman?

- Is there on the road academic support?

- What are the options besides the summer for student-athletes to study abroad?

- Do you have academic programs that support your athletes?

- If you have a diagnosed and documented disability (i.e. ADHD, ADD, etc.), what kind of academic services are available?

- Are there restrictions in scheduling classes around practice?

- How many credit hours can you take in-season and out-of-season?

- Is summer school available?

- If I need to take summer school, will it be paid for by the college?

Questions About Financial Aid

- How much financial aid is available for both the academic year and summer school?

- What does your scholarship cover?

- How long will the scholarship last?

- Can I work while playing sports?

- Where does community service fit into the team?

- What kinds of employment opportunities are available to me?

- Can I be employed in-season, out-of-season, or during vacation periods?

- What is not covered by the scholarship?

- What is the process to find out if I am eligible for financial aid?

- Would there be any restrictions to financial aid?

- Is there a GPA requirement to keep my athletic scholarship and/or financial aid?

- Have scholarships been canceled or reduced to players on your team? What were the circumstances?

- What is the school and your policy on the renewal of athletic scholarships and financial aid?

- Would my scholarship be affected if there is a change in coaches?

- If I suffer a career-ending injury, how is my athletic scholarship affected? Is there scholarship money available after eligibility is exhausted to allow me to complete my degree?

- Will I be signing a National Letter of Intent?

Questions for the Team

- Describe your typical day.

- How many hours a day do you put into athletics?

- How many hours a day are you in class?

- How many hours a day do you study?

- Describe your team culture.

- If you need to take classes for your major that conflict with practice, how does the coach handle that?

- Do you feel limited in your major or minor due to athletic requirements?

- Do you feel that you could study abroad if you wanted to?

- Does the coaching staff care about other parts of your life besides your athletic skills?

- Do you feel that all the athletes on the team are respected regardless of impact?

- Do you find it hard to balance sports and academics?

- Does your team athletic advisor meet with you regularly?

- How much information does the coach receive about missed class time and academic performance?

- What percentage of athletes will graduate in four years? Five years?

- Is there extra support in-season including free tutoring?

- What are the pros and cons of playing for the coach?

- Does the coach give honest assessments and good direction on how to improve as a player?

- Do you like the size of the college?

- What percentage of students live off campus?

- How many days in a row will the team be on the road? How do you handle academics on the road?

- How are freshman integrated into the team?

Kia McNeill
Head Coach Women's Soccer
2019 Coach of the Year / 2019 Ivy Champions
Brown University

DO spend some time with the players on campus when you go on a visit. 99% of your time as a college athlete is going to be spent with your teammates, and the general student body on campus. Spending time with the team can give you a sense of the team culture, their priorities, and generally what "a day in the life" is like for a student-athlete. Usually getting a gauge of the team culture and the vibe of the campus is what drives people towards or away from a school so these experiences are invaluable.

Takeaways

After your official or unofficial visit, take time to reflect on your impressions. Try to write it down within a day or two.

Did the staff and team seem to get along and care about each other?

How would you rate the team chemistry between the players and between players and staff?

How does the coach motivate the team?

Did you get a sense of how the coach motivates the team? How would you react to this style of coaching?

Were the coaches and staff friendly?

Did you feel like you established a relationship with the coaching team and staff during your visit? Did you feel like it was easy to get honest feedback about how you stand in their recruiting class?

Thank You Note

Be sure to send a thank you note or email after meeting with coaching staff on an official or unofficial visit. Reiterate in that note that you are interested in their program (assuming that you are) with specific examples based on your visit.

Sample Thank You Email After Meeting with Coaching Staff

Dear Coach Albermarle,

Thank you so much for having me this weekend. I loved the campus and the players were so warm and welcoming. It was powerful to see how your players put the team values into action. I really felt that WRAP resonated with me, and I now have a full sense of what it means to be a team player.

I also wanted to ask for some feedback regarding the camp on Sunday. Please let me know your thoughts whenever you can. I understand that you are busy in-season. Good luck in your game this weekend against Brown!

Go Huskies!

Best,

Alexandra Johnson '21
123 Anywhere Lane
Newton, MA 02468

AJohnson16@gmail.com
617-877-8777

Verbal Offers

The timeframe for verbal offers varies by Division. Division I and II schools make verbal offers sometime during the junior year. The timeline for Division III schools varies. Verbal offers will include the financial piece.

The parents of any PSA who is seriously being recruited in their junior year will be asked to submit the institution's financial aid paperwork for an "early read." The institutions will provide an estimate for the financial amount that the parents can expect based on the family's financial paperwork that was completed and submitted to the school. The financial estimate will be provided for all four years so that the family knows what they can expect to receive annually. This financial aid amount is split-up between family need-based aid (both grants and loans), academic grants, and other merit aid. This varies per institution since not all schools offer merit aid. This does NOT include any athletic related aid, IF the coach is thinking about offering that.

A financial aid early read generally happens once the player meets the school's academic requirements and is being actively recruited by the coach.

Schools often provide an early read within two weeks from the time the paperwork was submitted — provided the information was correct. Otherwise, financial aid will send an email requesting additional information. Unless the financial circumstances of the athlete's family changes, it should be an accurate assessment of what to expect from that school.

A verbal offer is not binding. There is no guarantee that a player who verbally commits to a team will end up there. A coach can change his or her mind about the prospect. The athlete may not have the academic qualifications to get accepted at the school. The coach may not be at that college when the athlete is ready to sign a binding offer, and the new coach might not honor the prior coach's verbal commitments.

This is the tricky stage of the recruiting process, in that athletes should have a back-up plan should the verbal offer not materialize into a binding written offer or come up short in terms of financial aid.

Maintaining communication with all the schools in play is important. Once you have accepted a verbal offer, be sure to close the loop with the other coaches and thank them for their time and interest.

You also want to get written confirmation of the verbal offer. For example, athletes can confirm the verbal offer that was communicated through a telephone conversation with a short email to thank the coach and relay how excited you are to commit to their program.

Verbal Financial Offers. Verbal financial offers and financial aid early reads are also non-binding. Only the scholarship amount contained in the official athletic grant-in-aid is binding. Remember, too, that scholarship commitments are only binding for one year though they are typically renewed each year.

Junior Year

- Update your list of colleges of interest (list should be narrowed down to 5-10 schools in the fall).

- Sign up for AP classes if possible as these could count towards college credits.

- Update your player profile with any new information (awards, GPA, SAT scores etc.) and **Focus on Grades!**

- Keep in touch with coaches once a month throughout the year.

- Fill out college questionnaires for prospective recruits and visit college fairs.

- Sign up for the SATS and ACT (www.collegeboard.com). Add scores to player profile.

- Stay in communication with coaches about upcoming showcases and interest in schools.

- Obtain at least three letters of recommendation or communicate with a club coach and ask for him or her to advocate.

- For financial aid, fill out the FAFSA form (www.fafsa. ed.gov) and attend workshops.

- Apply for the NCAA Eligibility Center (https://web3.ncaa. org/ecwr3).

- By the spring season narrow down your college list to a "Top 5-10 List".

- Attend College Night at your club or high school.

- Ask your high school counselor to send an official transcript to the NCAA Eligibility Center after completing your junior year.

- Attend four or five showcases a year (make sure to write to at least 10 coaches for each showcase).

- Go on unofficial visits (those which are financed entirely by the prospective student-athlete). DII, DIII, and NAIA unofficial visits are unlimited and can take place at any time. DI visits where you meet with the coaching staff cannot take place until August 1st of Junior year, but are then unlimited.

- DI and DII official college visits start on August 1st and are limited to five visits. DIII official visits are unlimited and start on January 15th.

- Attend College ID camps at schools of interest.

Lucy Jenks
Track and Field
Stanford University

When I visited Stanford, I really connected with the team and I had a lot of fun at my visit. I liked the area and the weather. Stanford also had the strongest track program out of all the colleges that I was looking at. I wanted to be on a team where I am really pushed and have to work my way up. I feel like this was the place that I wanted to be.

In running, it's a little different because you have to get into the school before the coach can offer you a scholarship. You submit the normal application through the athlete portal and wait to hear from Admissions. If you get accepted, then the coach can make a financial offer.

I had planned on applying to Stanford during the summer before my Senior year but then there was a coach change. Suddenly, there was no one there for me to be in contact with, so I didn't end up applying.

The coach change at Stanford added another level of stress especially because I didn't hear from him when the other three schools that I was talking to were trying to get me to commit. Some were more understanding about giving me more time than others, but one of the coaches gave me almost daily deadlines to respond or risk losing my money which was very stressful. That's when I talked to Alison Foley because I really didn't know how to handle that. She was the one who assured me that I was in control and that I needed to do what I want.

There was another girl who went on three visits with me. She also wanted to run at Stanford but she felt pressured to make her decision and committed to another school during the time when the new Stanford Track and Field coach was getting situated. After seeing other people wait it out and commit to Stanford, she ended up de-committing to that school, and committing to Stanford because that's where she really wanted to go. I didn't want that situation to happen to me so I told each coach that I wasn't ready to make my decision yet and I needed a little more time. I really did love the other schools but I wanted to have all my information before I made my final decision.

It also turns out that the initial offers that I received were not the final offers. By actually dragging out the process, my offers went up from 70% to 80% financial offers to close to full rides or actual full rides.

When the new coach was hired, he was busy getting to

know the team and hiring his staff which took him until about the beginning of October. I had already taken all my official visits and the other three coaches had offered me scholarships, but I waited to see if I would get into Stanford and what my offer would be. It was a stressful time. I loved the other schools but I knew that Stanford was my number one choice. The Stanford coach ended up flying out for a home visit and I really liked him. After meeting him, it made it easier to make my decision.

HIGH SCHOOL SENIOR YEAR

Keep your classwork up!

You are in the final home stretch and academics still matter! Finish strong! Your admission acceptance is official once the school has received your proof of graduation, which is your final transcript.

Narrow Your Search to Your Final School

By senior year, you have hopefully narrowed your search down to your final school and you have a clear idea of how the coach views you as part of your recruiting year team. If you are a top Division 1 athlete, you may have already committed. If not, let's keep going!

Where Do I Stand with the Coach?

It's important to get an honest assessment from the coach of where you stand in the recruiting class. Ask for this feedback. If you do not have a clear sense of where you stand after asking the coach where he or she sees your impact on the team, you will need to evaluate by other clues. How quickly does the coaching staff respond to you? If they have gone dark, that's not a good sign. Has a verbal offer been made? Have you been asked about an official visit?

Realize that there are different roles on the team. Perhaps the coach is interested in you but in a different role than the one you have in mind.

Players may move in and out of different roles depending on a number of factors such as injuries to players, graduating players, improvement, and incoming class.

The ball is in your court to ask for feedback from the coach, but you do need to persist to find out exactly where you stand.

Jojo Silagi

Men's Varsity Cross Country
Washington University in St. Louis

I started running cross country in sixth grade. I enjoyed running in high school but it wasn't my priority when it came to college. My college focus was centered around academics. It did happen that for most of the schools that I applied to, I would be able to run there, but I wasn't going out of my way to look at schools with running programs that I knew I could run at.

I chose Wash U with the expectation that I might not be running on a team in college. I knew that the cross country team here is very good, and I wouldn't have a guaranteed spot on the roster. And I was okay with that.

I did contact the coach at Wash U the summer before my senior year but we had limited communication. I let the coach know my times and that I was applying to Wash U. The coach wrote back to say that I should keep him updated on my times. When I was accepted at Wash U and knew that I would be going there, I wrote the coach again as a senior. The coach let me know that I would have to try out to make the team.

The summer before college, I kept running because it was what I wanted to do. The first week at college before the tryouts, I was still running. I wasn't explicitly running to train for tryouts, it was more just for the sake of running. I figured that I might as well go for it and see what happens. If I don't make the team, that's fine because I've already accepted that I might not make the team.

I ended up having a great tryout. The team had run the same course as the tryout the week prior as a time trial, and I had a faster time than some of the members of the team. I think that's what convinced the coach to give me a spot. I am currently the only walk-on on the team.

My coach made sure that I felt welcome as a walk-on. He's really amazing. I really admire and respect him. It was hard to get an impression of him before I got here because we were only emailing.

I really enjoyed my first college cross country season. The course is longer than in high school so that was an adjustment. I improved and stayed healthy. I am currently running indoor track in the winter and will run outdoor track in the spring. I plan to run for the next three years here.

The number one thing about running at a collegiate level is the people. I have grown so incredibly close to the other cross country team members, particularly the freshmen. I spend a lot of time with them not just at practice but also at meals and hanging out. They are all amazing. The team culture feels almost like family. And the athletic side has been amazing as well. I am being exposed to new training strategies and having fast people to run with helps me improve.

I would advise kids who are considering walking on to go for it. Do a little bit of training and just see if you can get the opportunity to try out. I think it's a really great experience to be on a sports team in college.

Juggling Multiple Schools Who Are Recruiting You

It may feel stressful to be actively recruited by multiple schools rather than just one. At this point, you are narrowing down your short list. As you make decisions, you will need to communicate to some coaches that they are no longer on your list. In this case, you can send a letter to officially decline.

Declining

The college sports world is a small one and you never know if you will run into the coaching staff again. Keep it polite and professional. Be sure to thank the coach for their time and interest. When possible, set up a phone call with the coach to decline.

Navigating a Verbal Commitment to a Written Commitment

You have received a verbal offer, gone on an official visit, expressed your interest to a coach for their college program, and now things have gone dark. This is the musical chairs portion of behind the scenes, in which coaches are sorting out the responses of their prospects.

Perhaps there are multiple candidates for your particular place on the team and they have not heard back from the person who may be one spot ahead of you. Perhaps the coaching staff has not reached a decision yet as they are still evaluating prospects.

The ranking decision of where you stand is out of your hands. However, you can express your interest in their program. You can also try to increase the urgency of a response if you have other offers from other colleges that perhaps come second to this school.

The key to turning the tide in your favor is patience, persistence, and professionalism. Express your interest but don't be annoying. Ask if there is a particular timeframe when a decision on you will be made. Let the coach know that you are willing to wait to hear from them before responding to the colleges that have made offers to you.

Even if a decision ultimately gets made that is not in your favor, be gracious and send a thank you note for their time.

These skills that you are learning in the final stretch of an offer will come in handy once you graduate from college and seek a full-time job. This is a life lesson that will pay dividends.

The Written Offer

The written offer is a one-year agreement that includes financial terms. For the majority of Division I and II, the signing date is November 14th. It's possible that the financial commitment can change over the four years though this is unusual. If your scholarship is going to increase over the four years, the NCAA now allows your NLI to be written over four years and you should request that.

Make Sure You Know the Application Requirements of the College

Be sure you meet both the NCAA or NAIA eligibility and college academic requirements.

Apply to College

You will still need to apply to the college that you are being recruited for. Check with the coach if you need to apply early or regular decision.

Early Read for NESCAC and Other Academic Conferences

The New England Small College Athletic Conference (NESCAC) is Division III and composed of Amherst College,

Bates College, Bowdoin College, Colby College, Connecticut College, Hamilton College, Middlebury College, Trinity College, Tufts College, Wesleyan College, and Williams College.

NESCAC coaches, as well as other Division III coaches, can submit athletes to Admissions for an academic early read which will indicate whether or not they can support the application. **They may be able to get a very good indication on your status on July 1st before your senior year.**

Social Media

Just as maintaining your academic performance is important to keep your place on the team, your social media presence is also being monitored. Don't assume that comments, posts, or membership to private groups will remain hidden. Conduct yourself online professionally and respectfully.

Keep the Coach Updated on Your Achievements

Continue to update the coach by sending them your revised resume though the fall. Keep training and playing at a high level. As seniors, you have accomplished your goal!

Congratulations! Your work has just begun now in terms of getting prepared to play and perform academically at the college level.

Information for Parents and Guardians

The recruitment rules can change so it's best to check with the umbrella organization to stay updated on the most current regulations. Some of these items pertain to NCAA schools only. This information is from NCAA.org.

Financial Aid

Athletic scholarships for Division I or II schools and financial aid for all colleges cover all or a portion of tuition and fees, room and board, and course-related books.

Here are some important things to know about athletic scholarships from Division I and II schools:

- Some athletic scholarship offers are limited to one year, but there are situations where a coach will offer a four year scholarship. The scholarship can be increased over the four years. If your scholarship is going to increase over the four years, the NCAA now allows your NLI to be written over four years and you should request that.

- On rare occasions, athletics aid can be canceled or reduced at the end of each year for any reason. If a school plans to reduce or not renew an athlete's aid, the school must notify the athlete in writing by July 1st and provide an opportunity to appeal. In most cases, it is the coach who decides who receives a scholarship, the amount of the scholarship, and whether it will be renewed. A non-renewal is not based on injury or performance but more likely poor academic standing or a significant behavior infraction.

- Athletics scholarships may be renewed annually for a maximum of five years within a six-year period of continuous college attendance.

- Athletics scholarships are awarded in a variety of amounts, ranging from full scholarships (including tuition, fees, room, board and books) to very small scholarships that, for example, provides only required course-related books.

- The total amount of financial aid a student-athlete may receive and the total amount of athletic scholarships a team may receive can be limited. These limits can affect whether an athlete may accept additional financial aid from other sources. Ask financial aid officials as well as the coach at the college or university about other financial aid you may be eligible to receive and about the impact of that aid on athletics aid limits.

- An athletic scholarship can help to cover the cost of college, but may not include costs such as travel between home and school. However, there are Pell Grants that can be requested through the financial aid department that can help students who cannot afford travel home or other necessary items such as clothing and items for your dorm room. There is also international student-athlete money which can also assist in travel home during certain times of the year. This is not always available at all schools.

- Always have a plan of how to finance your education if your athletic scholarship is canceled or reduced.

For information on financial aid at NAIA schools:

www.naia.org/membership/2017-18/releases/financial-aid

Applying for Financial Aid: FAFSA

FAFSA (Free Application for Federal Student Aid) is a form used by current and prospective college students in the U.S. to determine their eligibility for student financial aid. In addition to FAFSA, some colleges also require the CSS profile. The FAFSA determines a family's estimated contribution, thus how much financial aid the student can receive.

For a ballpark estimation of your estimated financial contribution, FinAid.org has an Expected Family Contribution Calculator **https://www.finaid.org/calculators/** as well as a Quick Expected Family Calculator **https://www.finaid.org/calculators/quickefc.phtml.**

Even if you might not receive a significant amount of financial aid, it's worth completing the FAFSA because it can act as an insurance policy in case there is a change or loss of income in your family. You will not be eligible for college financial aid if you do not complete the FAFSA on an annual basis.

To complete the FAFSA online, go to **www.fafsa.ed.gov**. You can obtain a FSA ID to electronically sign the form from **https://studentaid.ed.gov/sa/fafsa/filling-out/fsaid**. For technical questions about the FAFSA website, call 1-800-FED-AID.

The first date you may submit the FAFSA is January 1st of senior year. Submit the FAFSAS on this date or as close to the date as possible!

University financial aid budgets are awarded on a first come first served basis, so the earlier you submit your FAFSA, the better! Each college/university has a specific deadline and at a certain point, the money does run out.

National Letter of Intent (NLI)

The National Letter of Intent is a voluntary program administered by the NCAA Eligibility Center, and is only issued when a PSA is offered some type of athletic scholarship. When you sign the NLI, your child agrees to attend the institution for one academic year. Signing dates for NLI are here: **http://www.nationalletter.org/signingDates/index.html**

If you have questions about the NLI call 317-223-0706 or visit the NLI Web site at **www.national-letter.org**

Agents

During high school, agents may contact your child and show interest in representing them, but while NCAA rules do not prevent meeting or talking to an agent, current rules prohibit athletes, with the exception of Men's Basketball, from entering into an agreement with an agent or receiving any benefits from an agent at any time. This includes entering an agreement that does not take effect until after their last season of college eligibility. Accepting gifts, either by the athlete or parent, can also jeopardize college eligibility.

2019 new rules applying to Men's Basketball are here: **https:// ncaaorg.s3.amazonaws.com/enforcement/2019ENF_ NBAMemo.pdf**

DISASTER SCENARIOS

It's possible that everything was going well, but now the worst case scenario has happened, turning the commitment to a college program on its head. While a disaster scenario feels like everything that the athlete has worked for is slipping away, all is not lost. There is a fix for every disaster scenario.

Long Term Injury

Perhaps the timing could not be worse. The athlete gets a long-term injury after getting a verbal offer but before signing an official offer. How will this affect the chances of receiving an athletic scholarship now?

The good news is that not all injuries are career ending. Injuries heal and your child's ability to perform his or her sport at a high level is not obliterated; it's just on hold. Obviously, the primary goal is to get the athlete well again. Let the coaching staff know about the injury. Perhaps they have resources to suggest for recovery. The player should keep the college coach updated with medical updates and progress reports.

This will be a character check for the coaching staff. They are not legally bound to have the athlete sign a National Letter of Intent (NLI) after a verbal commitment. Hopefully, you have determined that they are a trustworthy coaching staff that will continue to support the athlete and their offer.

Coach I Committed To is No Longer at that College

If the coach gave a verbal commitment but now is no longer at that college, it's important to find out if the verbal commitment will be honored and will materialize into a written offer. This can be tricky because there may be a period of time when the college is seeking a head coach replacement. The new hire may need to begin the evaluation process all over again. A private athletic recruiter could be helpful, especially if there isn't much time left before formal written offers will be made. You should contact the Athletic Director at the institution and find out the rule on commitments. They ultimately decide whether or not the offers have to be honored.

Verbal Commitment is Not Materializing to a Written Commitment

Perhaps the coach has stopped responding after making a verbal offer and after months of emails and calls, the athlete has not heard anything. Clearly, something has gone sideways.

Alternately, the student is confused as to how he or she stands in the recruiting class. Perhaps the coach is ambiguous. The high school or club coach should step in at this point for clarification. A private athletic college counselor could be also helpful in reading between the lines.

If the coach does not seem like he or she will extend a written offer, it's time to 1) come up with a list of colleges that are similar to this one, and 2) talk to the coaches on this new list. The athlete may not have necessarily been talking to the coaches on this new list but that's okay. Finding the right fit for level of play and academics can be a trial and error experience. While this might feel like a disaster scenario, the athlete might actually be one college coach away from finding a home.

The athlete, parents, coach, and college counselor should work together to come up with a back-up plan. Private sports college counselors might also be helpful at this stage.

Admission Fail

It's important to understand if there is a particular admission issue. Are all the prerequisites for admission to that college completed? If something is missing, will Admissions allow for a summer make-up class prior to starting college?

If the issue is GPA or SAT scores, there isn't much runway to address that. If there is no work around an admission fail, it's time to talk to coaches who expressed interest and whose college admission standards are less competitive. A private athletic recruiter could be helpful in this scenario to explore more possibilities in a tight timeframe. Be sure to interview and get specifics about what they can do in this situation.

Senior Year

- Improve your SAT/ACT scores if possible by retaking tests (December is the latest for testing)

- Update your list of colleges of interest (list should be narrowed down to five schools at most)

- Stay in communication with schools at least once a month and continue to go on unofficial visits

- Official visits (five in total for Division I and II / unlimited for Division III)

- Sign up for AP classes, if possible, as these will count towards college credits

- Update your player profile with any new information (awards, GPA, SAT scores, etc.)

- Focus on grades

- Apply to your school of choice

- Signing day is in November; however seniors can sign a National Letter of Intent up until August 1st

- Finalize recommendation letters, financial aid applications (January 1st), and essays

- Obtain final transcripts from your counselor (when applicable)

- Make sure you meet all deadlines for applications, housing, scholarships, etc.

- Send final transcripts to the NCAA Clearinghouse

COACHES' BIOGRAPHIES

Sarah Dacey, Head Coach of Women's Soccer, Barry University

Sarah joined Barry University as Head Coach in 2016 after spending the previous season as an Assistant Coach under Denise Brolly. Formerly, Dacey was the Head Coach at Babson College, as well as Club Head with FC Bolts and Pinecrest Premier Soccer Club. She served as an Assistant Coach at the University of Albany, Providence College, the University of Tennessee, and Boston College, where she helped lead the Eagles to the 2010 Women's College Cup.

Dacey played professionally for the WUSA's Carolina Courage and the Boston Breakers until 2003. A four-year letter winner and three-year starter under Anson Dorrance at UNC, Dacey helped lead the Tar Heels' soccer program to three National Championships while earning Honorable Mention All-American honors in 1996.

Gregory DiCenzo, Head Coach of Men's Baseball, College of the Holy Cross

Greg DiCenzo became Head Coach of Men's Baseball at Holy Cross in 2008. Under his guidance, Holy Cross won its first Patriot League Championship in program history in 2017, and the Crusaders have made four additional Patriot League championship series appearances in 2010, 2012, 2013 and 2016. DiCenzo was named Patriot League Coach of the Year in 2008 and 2013, and is the third highest winning coach in program history, ranking seventh in all-time in victories. After twelve seasons with Holy Cross, Dicenzo resigned and is currently the manager of the Class A Lake County Captains in the Cleveland Indians organization.

DiCenzo earned three degrees from St. Lawrence University with a Bachelor of Science Degree (1998), a Master's Degree in Education (2000) and a Master's Degree in Education Administration (2002). He spent four seasons on the baseball coaching staff at his alma mater – three as an assistant coach and one as an interim head coach – and two seasons as an assistant football coach. As an athlete, DiCenzo was a four-year member of the St. Lawrence baseball team, captaining the team as a senior. He was also a one-year member of St. Lawrence's men's soccer team, and a four-time All-Conference kicker and punter for the school's football team.

Kelly Doton, Head Coach of Women's Field Hockey, Boston College

Kelly Doton became Head Coach of the Boston College field hockey program in 2015. She started as the Associate Head Coach at Boston College in 2012, having previously coached at Indiana University. In her first two seasons at the program's helm, Doton led the Eagles to back-to-back NCAA Tournament appearances in 2015 and 2016. In 2019, Doton brought BC to new heights, leading the Eagles to 15 wins, with a program-record four ACC wins, and was named the ACC Coach of the Year. She then led the Eagles on a postseason run that saw BC make its first final four in program history.

A 2004 graduate of Wake Forest, Doton was named the ACC Player of the year in 2002, and was a two-time NFHCA First Team All-American and a three-time All-ACC honoree during her career. Doton was a member of the U.S. Women's Senior National Team from 2005-2010. In 2008, she was part of the U.S. squad that traveled to the Summer Olympics in Beijing, China.

John Kennaday, Head Coach of Men's Golf, San Jose State University

John Kennaday returned to San Jose State University, his alma mater, as Head Coach of Men's Golf in 2005. Under his watch, San Jose State opened a 15-acre on-campus practice facility in 2017 that allows players to work on every facet of the game. As the head coach of the Spartans, San Jose State has NCAA Regional Championship appearances as a team in 2011, 2012 and 2019. In 2012, he was named the Western Athletic Conference (WAC) Coach of the Year after leading the Spartans to a conference championship and three more tournament victories that season. Previously, Kennaday spent seven seasons as the Head Coach for the Santa Clara University men's golf team.

As a player, Kennaday was a two-time Coast Conference Most Valuable Player at Monterey Peninsula College before transferring to San Jose State where he earned All-American honors in 1987. He was a 1986 and 1987 first-team All-Pacific Coast Athletic Association (PCAA) pick, and helped the Spartans to a 12th-place tie at the 1987 NCAA Championships. He went on to play professionally on the Canadian PGA, Nike, and Golden State Tours for seven-plus years.

Peter Kim, Head Coach of Women's Soccer, Assistant Coach of Men's and Women's Track and Field, Middlebury College

Kim has taken the Women's Soccer team at Middlebury to nine NCAA Tournaments. The Panthers have advanced to the NESCAC Championship match four times in his tenure, taking home the title in 2006, 2013 and 2018. He has been named the NESCAC Coach of the Year on six different occasions (2004, 2006, 2009, 2012, 2013, 2018).

Kim played college soccer at the University of Vermont from

1989-92. In 2001, he was honored with the "Outstanding Contributor to Youth Soccer" award by the Vermont Soccer Coaches Association. That year, he co-founded the Vermont Amateur Soccer League, to raise the level of adult play while developing a unique soccer mentoring program to connect adult and youth teams in the area. Currently, he directs Capital Soccer, a soccer education organization in central Vermont, and is Director of Coaching and Player Development for the Capital Soccer Club.

Kia McNeill, Head Coach of Women's Soccer, Brown University

McNeill was named Brown's Head Women's Soccer Coach on December 30, 2015. Under her guidance, she led the Bears to a record of .500 or better in each of her first three seasons. As an Assistant Coach at Northeastern in the 2014 and 2015 seasons and at Boston College in 2009 and the 2011-13 seasons, McNeill helped those two programs make five NCAA tournament appearances in six seasons, including an Elite Eight and three Sweet 16 appearances at BC.

McNeill was the National Gatorade Player of the Year in 2004 and a two-time NSCAA High School All-American at Avon High School. As a collegiate student-athlete, McNeill played at BC from 2004-07, earning Big East Rookie of the Year accolades in 2004 and Third Team All-America honors as a senior. McNeill played professional women's soccer for six seasons (2008-14) both internationally and in the United States. She was the No. 9 pick in the inaugural WPS draft in 2009 and finished her career with the Boston Breakers of the NWSL in 2013-14.

ADDITIONAL RESOURCES

Scholarship Resource for Women

The Official Athletic College Guide: Over 1,300 Women's Scholarships Listed

Scholarship Search Engines

https://www.fastweb.com/college-scholarships

https://www.scholarships.com/

https://jlvcollegecounseling.com/scholarships/

Scholarship Search Engines that also do College Matching

https://www.collegeweeklive.com/

https://www.chegg.com/scholarships

https://www.collegegreenlight.com/

Scholarship for Minorities

Jackie Robinson Foundation Scholarship:
www.jackierobinson.org/apply/

Scholarships for African American Students

Gates Millennium Scholars Program: https://gmsp.org/

The Ron Brown Scholar Program: www.ronbrown.org

UNCF/Merck Undergraduate Science Research Scholarship:
https://gs.columbia.edu/uncf-merck-undergraduate-science-research-scholarship-awards

https://scholarships.uncf.org/

HBCU Forever Site: https://hbcuforever.org/scholarship-opportunities/

Scholarship Search for Hispanic Students

https://lulac.org/programs/education/scholarships/

Scholarships for First Generation or Disadvantaged Students

Jack Kent Cooke Foundation Scholarships:
www.jkcf.org/our-scholarships/

Posse Foundation: www.possefoundation.org

Nonprofit Dedicated to Increasing the number of Native American, Alaska Native, and Native Hawaiian students in college and graduate programs

https://collegehorizons.publishpath.com/default.
aspx?OriginalDomain=www.collegehorizons.org

Resources for Undocumented Students or Parents

Financial Aid for Undocumented Students or Parents

Colleges that Meet 100% of Financial Need for Undocumented Students

Scholarships for Undocumented Students

Online College Fairs or Visits

www.collegeweeklive.com/

Video College Tours

www.youniversitytv.com/

Colleges with Great Financial Aid

From Money.com: These 75 Colleges Promise to Meet 100% of Students' Financial Need: https://money.com/colleges-that-meet-full-financial-need/

From US News and World Report: Most Students Receiving Merit Aid: www.usnews.com/best-colleges/rankings/most-merit-aid

Colleges with "No Loan" Financial Aid Programs (for certain types of students)

www.finaid.org/questions/noloansforlowincome.phtml

Colleges that Don't Require SAT or ACT Scores

www.fairtest.org/sites/default/files/Optional-Schools-in-U.S.News-Top-Tiers.pdf

www.fairtest.org/university/optional

Application and Essay Tips from Ethan Sawyer, The College Essay Guy

Supplemental Essays – "Why This College" Essay Guide + Examples

University of California Application Resources

Majors and Careers

https://collegemajors101.com/

https://bigfuture.collegeboard.org/majors-careers (info on majors and careers)

https://www.bls.gov/ooh/ (had median pay, growth outlook, and degree requirement for jobs)

ABOUT THE AUTHORS

Alison Foley

Alison Foley was Boston College's Women's Soccer Head Coach for more than 20 years. During her tenure, she was BC's highest winning coach, with more than 260 victories. She led her team to the NCAA Final Four, and Final Eight during 13 consecutive play-off appearances. In her 20+ year career, she coached many national team level players. She is currently the founder of Foley Athletic Advising, which provides expertise in the college recruiting process for student-athletes who aspire to play in college. She co-wrote *How To Coach Girls* with Mia Wenjen.

Mia Wenjen

Mia Wenjen blogs on education and children's books at Pragmatic Mom.com. She is the co-creator of Multicultural Children's Book Day, a non-profit dedicated to getting diversity books into the hands of readers, and co-founder of Aquent, a staffing company specializing in placing temporary employees in marketing and creative industries. She is the author of the anthology *Best #OwnVoices Children's Books*, middle grade non-fiction *Asian Pacific American Heroes*, and picture book *Sumo Joe*. This is her second book co-authored with Alison Foley.

INDEX

ACKNOWLEDGEMENTS

This book would not be possible without the insights and editing talents of Tai Lee, Marco Koolman, Sidnie Kulik, Ali Lee, and Lydia Davis. Tai Lee earned a full-ride scholarship at the University of Hawaii where he played on the men's golf team. Marco Koolman, the Head Coach of men's soccer at Holy Cross, was our patient fact checker. Sidnie Kulik, a multi-sport athlete, brought the student-athlete perspective to our book. Ali Lee was our lookout for grammatical errors. Thank you also to our amazing editor, Lydia Davis, who returns having previously edited *How To Coach Girls*.

Thank you also to Sam Apuzzo, Kevin Belzer, Sophie Bengochea, Jude Braithwaite, Jacob Jampel, Lucy Jenks, Steph McCaffrey, and Jojo Solage, who are a source of inspiration in their journeys as athletes, students, and human beings.

Finally, a huge thank you to coaches Sarah Dacey and Kelly Doton who provided insights for *How To Coach Girls* and still agreed to help out with our newest book. Thank you also to coaches Gregory DiCenzo, John Kennaday, Peter Kim, and Kia McNeill for their sharing front-line advice on college athletic recruiting.

NOTES